DISCARDED

Vital Records Handbook

DISCARDED

DISCARDED

Vital Records Handbook

Thomas J. Kemp

Assistant Director, Pequot Library
Southport, Connecticut

GENEALOGICAL PUBLISHING CO., INC.
Baltimore 1989

DISCARDED

Copyright © 1988 by
Thomas J. Kemp
All Rights Reserved
Published by Genealogical Publishing Co., Inc.
Baltimore, 1988, 1989
Library of Congress Catalogue Card Number 88-80164
International Standard Book Number 0-8063-1220-3
Made in the United States of America

CONTENTS

Dedicated to my wife, Vi

INTRODUCTION

At one time or another all of us will need copies of birth, marriage, or death certificates for such necessities as driver's licenses, passports, jobs, or social security. The *Vital Records Handbook* is designed to make it as easy as possible to obtain copies of these records.

The book is divided into three parts: (1) the United States; (2) United States Trust Territories; and (3) selected foreign countries. The District of Columbia is included with the states. The foreign countries include Canada, Ireland, and the United Kingdom (England and Wales, Scotland, and Northern Ireland).

The application forms issued by the various record offices and the current procedures for obtaining a birth, marriage, or death certificate are given for each state, province, territory, or country. Simply photocopy the form you need, follow the instructions, and send the fee and the completed form to the appropriate record office.

Regulations and fees often change, as do the application forms, and the author would be grateful to learn of such changes as the reader becomes aware of them.

ALABAMA

Send your requests to:

Alabama Department of Public Health
Bureau of Vital Statistics
State Office Building
501 Dexter Avenue
Montgomery, Alabama 36130-1701

(205) 261-5033

Cost for a certified Birth Certificate	$5.00
Cost for a certified Marriage Certificate	$5.00
Cost for a certified Death Certificate	$5.00
Cost for a duplicate copy, when ordered at the same time	$2.00

Birth and death records are on file at the State Office from January 1908. Births are filed under the father's name by the date and place the event occurred. Marriage records are on file from August 1, 1936. NO PERSONAL CHECKS ARE ACCEPTED. Send a money order payable to "Alabama State Board of Health."

If your request is urgent you may call and charge your certificates to your visa or mastercard. There is an $18.50 charge for this service.

ALABAMA DEPARTMENT OF PUBLIC HEALTH—VITAL STATISTICS
APPLICATION FOR BIRTH RECORD

TYPE OR PRINT
DATE: _____

Full name: _____
First   Middle   Last

Date of birth: _____ Sex: _____

Place of birth: _____
Hospital   City   County

This was the _____ child born to this mother. Is this an adopted child? _____
1st, 2nd, 3rd, 4th, etc.

What changes are you requesting? _____

Next older sister of brother _____ Younger _____

Full name of father _____ / _____
First   Middle   Last   Race

Full maiden name of mother _____ / _____
First   Middle   Last (Maiden)   Race

AMOUNT ENCLOSED $ _____ (NO PERSONAL CHECKS ACCEPTED)

MAIL RECORD TO:

Name: _____

Street: _____

City or Town: _____
Zip

Signature of person making request: _____

DO NOT TEAR

DO NOT WRITE IN THESE SPACES
(File Number)
Additional information requested
Evidence Requested
Amendment Form Mailed
Informational letter mailed
Advised record not on file
CERTIFIED COPY ISSUED

DO NOT WRITE IN THIS SPACE

THIS WILL BE YOUR RECEIPT AFTER WE PROCESS IT AND RETURN IT TO YOU.

Certificate of _____

(This is a mailing insert. PRINT name and address of person to whom the certified copy is to be mailed)

MAIL TO:

Name: _____

Street: _____

City or Town: _____
Zip

DO NOT TEAR   (TYPE OR PRINT)

MAIL TO:

Name: _____

Street: _____

City or Town: _____
Zip

ADPH-F-VS-14/Rev. 10-84

MAIL APPLICATION TO:

ALABAMA DEPARTMENT OF PUBLIC HEALTH
BUREAU OF VITAL STATISTICS
STATE OFFICE BUILDING
MONTGOMERY, ALABAMA 36130-1701

ALABAMA DEPARTMENT OF PUBLIC HEALTH—VITAL STATISTICS
APPLICATION FOR MARRIAGE RECORD

TYPE OR PRINT

Full name of groom_____
First   Middle   Last

Birthday of groom _____ Color or Race _____

Groom's Mother _____
First   Middle   Last (Maiden name)

Groom's Father _____
First   Middle   Last

Full name of bride_____
First   Middle   Last

Birthday of bride _____ Color or Race _____

Bride's Mother _____
First   Middle   Last (Maiden name)

Bride's Father _____
First   Middle   Last

License obtained in _____
County   State

Date of marriage_____
Month   Day   Year

Place of marriage_____
City   County   State

AMOUNT ENCLOSED $ _____ (NO PERSONAL CHECKS ACCEPTED)

Signature of person making request: _____

Street: _____

City or Town: _____
Zip

- -
DO NOT TEAR

Fees must be paid in advance and are not refundable. Payment should be made by MONEY ORDER payable to the State Board of Health.

DO NOT SEND CASH. NO PERSONAL CHECKS ACCEPTED.

(DO NOT WRITE IN THESE SPACES)

(File Number)

Additional information requested

Evidence Requested

_____

_____

Amendment Form Mailed

_____

Informational letter mailed

_____

Advised record not on file

CERTIFIED COPY ISSUED

(DO NOT WRITE IN THIS SPACE)
(Validating machine only)

MAIL TO: Name: _____

Street: _____

City or Town: _____
Zip

- -
DO NOT TEAR   (TYPE OR PRINT)

MAIL TO: SEND TO:

Name: _____

Street: _____

City or Town: _____
Zip

ALABAMA DEPARTMENT OF PUBLIC HEALTH
BUREAU OF VITAL STATISTICS
STATE OFFICE BUILDING
MONTGOMERY, ALABAMA 36130

ADPH-F-VS-12/Rev. 6-80

ALABAMA DEPARTMENT OF PUBLIC HEALTH—VITAL STATISTICS
APPLICATION FOR DEATH RECORD

TYPE OR PRINT

Full name of deceased _____
First   Middle   Last

Date of death _____ Age: _____ Sex: _____ Race: _____

Place of death _____
City   County

Name of
Husband or Wife _____
First   Middle   Last

Name of Funeral Home _____

Full Name of Father _____
First   Middle   Last

Full maiden name of mother _____
First   Middle   Last (Maiden)

AMOUNT ENCLOSED $ _____ NUMBER OF COPIES _____
(NO PERSONAL CHECKS ACCEPTED)

MAIL RECORD TO:

Name: _____

Street: _____

City or Town: _____
Zip

Signature of person making request: _____

DO NOT TEAR

DO NOT WRITE IN THIS SPACE
File No.
Additional Information Requested
Evidence Requested
Amendment Form Mailed
Informational Letter Mailed
Advised Record Not On File
Certified Copy Issued

DO NOT SEND CASH. NO PERSONAL CHECKS ACCEPTED.

MAIL TO:

Name: _____

Street: _____

City or Town: _____
Zip

DO NOT REMOVE THIS STUB ⬆

TYPE OR PRINT MAILING ADDRESS ON BOTH INSERTS
⬇

DO NOT WRITE IN THIS SPACE

THIS WILL BE YOUR RECEIPT AFTER WE PROCESS IT AND RETURN IT TO YOU.

MAIL TO:

Name: _____

Street: _____

City or Town: _____
Zip

MAIL APPLICATION TO:

ALABAMA DEPARTMENT OF PUBLIC HEALTH
BUREAU OF VITAL STATISTICS
STATE OFFICE BUILDING
MONTGOMERY, ALABAMA 36130-1701

ADPH-F-VS-18/Rev. 10-84

ALASKA

Send your requests to:

Bureau of Vital Statistics
Alaska Department of Health and Social Services
P.O. Box H
Juneau, Alaska 99811

(907) 465-3393

Cost for a certified Birth Certificate	$5.00
Cost for a plastic Birth Certificate	$5.00
Cost for a certified Marriage Certificate	$5.00
Cost for a certified Death Certificate	$5.00
Cost for a duplicate copy, when ordered at the same time	$2.00

The State Bureau of Vital Statistics has records from January 1913.

If your request is urgent you may call and charge your certificates to your visa or mastercard. There is a $5.00 fee for this service.

Application for Certification of a Vital Event

DEPARTMENT OF HEALTH AND SOCIAL SERVICES   BUREAU OF VITAL RECORDS
Pouch H — Juneau, Alaska 99811

Type of Event
(Please check one)

___ BIRTH   ___ DEATH   ___ MARRIAGE   ___ DIVORCE

Facts Concerning the Vital Record

FULL NAME _____

(First)   (Middle)   (Last)

_____

DATE OF EVENT   PLACE OF EVENT

_____

(if a birth) NAME OF FATHER   (if a birth) MAIDEN NAME OF MOTHER

Certification

NUMBER OF COPIES WANTED   TYPE AND FEE

	Certified photocopy
	Plastic Birth Card, billfold size (BIRTHS ONLY)

Money orders, made out to the BUREAU OF VITAL STATISTICS, are preferred   TOTAL $_____

PURPOSE FOR WHICH NEEDED _____

Applicant

SIGNATURE OF APPLICANT _____ DATE _____

MAILING ADDRESS _____
CITY, STATE AND ZIP CODE

RELATIONSHIP TO PERSON WHOSE RECORD IS BEING REQUESTED_____

WHERE TO MAIL THIS FORM

If the event occurred in Alaska
mail this form and the proper fee to:

Bureau of Vital Statistics
Alaska Department of Health and Social Services
P.O. Box H
Juneau, Alaska 99811

Important:

*Please print the address to which
certification is to be sent
in this space*

>

ARIZONA

Send your requests to:

Office of Vital Records
Arizona Department of Health Services
1740 West Avenue
P.O. Box 3887
Phoenix, Arizona 85030-3887

(602) 255-1072

Send your requests for Marriage Certificates to:

Clerk
Superior Court
(County where the Marriage License was issued)

Cost for a certified Birth Certificate	$5.00
Cost for a short form Birth Certificate	$3.00
Cost for a plastic Birth Certificate	$5.00
Cost for a certified Death Certificate	$3.00

The Arizona Office of Vital Records began keeping records in July of 1909. They do have abstracts of some records filed in the County Clerk's Offices before that date. Your request must be accompanied by a copy of a photo ID card witnessed by a notary public. Payment must be by a certified check or money order.

If your request is urgent you may call and charge your certificates to your visa or mastercard. There is a $4.50 fee for this service.

ARIZONA DEPARTMENT OF HEALTH SERVICES
VITAL RECORDS SECTION

REQUEST FOR COPY OF BIRTH CERTIFICATE

☐ COUNTER
☐ MAIL

DATE _____

ENCLOSED $ _____ IN _____ FOR _____
AMOUNT   CASH, CHECK, ETC.

SPECIFY: CERTIFIED (LONG FORM); BIRTH CARD; OR SHORT FORM

☐ Certified Copy (Long Form)
☐ Plastic Birth Card
☐ Computer (Short Form)

I. BIRTH CERTIFICATE OF:

FULL NAME AT BIRTH

DATE OF BIRTH   SEX

PLACE OF BIRTH (City, County, State, Hospital)

MOTHER'S MAIDEN NAME (First, Middle, Last)   MOTHER'S BIRTHPLACE

HOSPITAL OR FACILITY

FATHER'S FULL NAME   FATHER'S BIRTHPLACE

For the protection of the individual, certificates of vital events are NOT open to public inspection. The following MUST BE COMPLETED in order to permit this office to comply with the request.

WARNING: False application for a birth certificate is a punishable offense.

II. PERSON MAKING REQUEST

Your Signature ☞

YOUR NAME

YOUR ADDRESS (Number and Street)

(Town, State)   (Zip Code)

RELATIONSHIP TO PERSON NAMED IN CERTIFICATE (e.g., parent, attorney, etc.)

FOR WHAT PURPOSE DO YOU NEED THIS COPY?

TELEPHONE NO. (Optional)

Send completed application and correct fee to
OFFICE OF VITAL RECORDS
Arizona Department of
Health Services
P.O. Box 3887
Phoenix, Arizona 85030

FOR OFFICE USE ONLY

DATE ISSUED

STATE FILE NUMBER

DATE FILED

ADHS/ADM/Vital Records
VS-15A (Rev. 3-84)

ARIZONA DEPARTMENT OF HEALTH SERVICES
OFFICE OF VITAL RECORDS

APPLICATION FOR COPY OF DEATH CERTIFICATE

☐ COUNTER

☐ MAIL

DATE			
ENCLOSED $ _____ IN _____ FOR _____ COPIES OF THE FOLLOWING DEATH CERTIFICATE:			
AMOUNT	CASH, CHECK, ETC		

Please do not send cash. Make check or money order payable to Arizona Department of Health Services.

1 NAME OF DECEASED - First, Middle, Last

IF ANOTHER LAST NAME (except by marriage) WAS EVER USED, ENTER HERE

2 DATE OF DEATH - Month, Day, Year | SEX | SOCIAL SECURITY NUMBER (necessary for positive identification)

3 PLACE OF DEATH - Hospital or Residence | Town or City | County | **ARIZONA**

4 IF MARRIED IS WIFE/HUSBAND OF DECEASED NOW LIVING? ☐ YES ☐ NO

IF YES, LIST NAME - First Middle Last

5 HOW WILL COPIES BE USED?

ARE COPIES TO BE USED FOR U.S. GOV'T CLAIMS? ☐ YES ☐ NO

IF YES, LIST EACH TYPE OF CLAIM

6. **SIGNATURE OF APPLICANT (The regulations require a signed application)**

WHAT IS YOUR RELATIONSHIP TO THE DECEASED?

7 TYPE OR PRINT NAME AND CORRECT MAIL ADDRESS BELOW

NAME

STREET ADDRESS OR P.O. BOX NUMBER

CITY AND STATE | ZIP CODE

SEND COMPLETED APPLICATION AND CORRECT FEE TO:
OFFICE OF VITAL RECORDS
Arizona Dept. of Health Services
P.O. Box 3887
Phoenix, AZ 85030-3887

FOR OFFICE USE ONLY

STATE FILE NUMBER

DATE ISSUED

REMARKS

ADHS/ADM/Vital Records and Information Services-15B (Rev. 8-81)

ARKANSAS

Send your requests to:

Arkansas Department of Health
Division of Vital Records
4815 West Markham Street
Little Rock, Arkansas 72205-3867

(501) 661-2371

Cost for a certified Birth Certificate	$5.00
Cost for a certified Marriage Certificate	$5.00
Cost for a certified Death Certificate	$4.00

The Arkansas Department of Health began filing birth and death records February 1, 1914 and marriage records January 1, 1917. They do have some birth records for individuals that were filed as delayed certificates.

If your request is urgent you may call and charge your certificates to your visa or mastercard. There is a $4.50 charge for this service.

DATE _____

APPLICATION FOR CERTIFIED COPY OF CERTIFICATE OF BIRTH

Only Arkansas births are recorded in this office. There are no original birth records for events which occurred before February 1, 1914. The fee is per certificate copy or birth registration card. This fee must accompany the application. Send check or money order payable to the Arkansas Department of Health. DO NOT SEND CASH. Of the total fee you send, $5.00 will be kept in this office to cover search charges if no record of the birth is found.

INFORMATION ABOUT PERSON WHOSE BIRTH CERTIFICATE IS REQUESTED (Type or Print)				
1. FULL NAME AT BIRTH	FIRST NAME	MIDDLE NAME		LAST NAME
2. DATE OF BIRTH	MONTH / DAY / YEAR		SEX & RACE	AGE LAST BIRTHDAY
3. PLACE OF BIRTH	CITY OR TOWN / COUNTY / STATE			ORDER OF THIS BIRTH (1st, 2nd, 3rd, etc.)
	NAME OF HOSPITAL OR STREET ADDRESS		ATTENDANT AT BIRTH	
4. FULL NAME OF FATHER	FIRST NAME	MIDDLE NAME		LAST NAME
5. FULL MAIDEN NAME OF MOTHER (NAME BEFORE MARRIAGE)	FIRST NAME	MIDDLE NAME		MAIDEN NAME

If this child has been adopted, please give original name if known.

_____

Has a copy of this certificate been received before? _____

If this is a delayed certificate, when was it filed? _____

What is your relationship to the person whose certificate is being requested?

_____

What is your reason for requesting this certificate? _____

_____

Is the person whose record is being requested still living? _____

If the birth was not recorded, do you wish to file a delayed birth record? _____

Signature and telephone number of person requesting this certificate:

_____

DO NOT WRITE IN THIS SPACE	
Searcher	
Index	
Delayed	Prior
Volume No.	
Page No.	Yr.

DO NOT DETACH

Please **PRINT** below the name and address of the person who is to receive the copy(s) or card(s).

THERE ARE TWO TYPES OF CERTIFICATE COPIES AVAILABLE:
(1) A PAPER COPY, AND, (2) A PLASTIC, BILLFOLD-SIZE BIRTH CARD WITHOUT NAMES OF PARENTS.
BOTH TYPES OF COPIES ARE LEGAL PROOF OF THE EVENT OF BIRTH.

COPIES REQUESTED	
PAPER COPY	HOW MANY ☐
BIRTH CARD	HOW MANY ☐
AMOUNT OF MONEY ENCLOSED	$

_____

_____

ZIP

VR-7 A—3702

Any person who willfully and knowingly makes any false statement in an application for a certified copy of a vital record filed in this state is subject to a fine of not more than ten thousand dollars ($10,000) or imprisoned not more than five (5) years, or both. (Ark. Statutes 82-527).

DATE _____

**ARKANSAS DEPARTMENT OF HEALTH
DIVISION OF VITAL RECORDS
4815 WEST MARKHAM STREET
LITTLE ROCK, ARKANSAS 72205-3867**

APPLICATION FOR CERTIFIED COPY OF MARRIAGE OR DIVORCE RECORD

Only Arkansas events of marriage or divorce are filed in this office. Marriage records start with 1917 and divorce records with 1923. The fee is per certified copy of a marriage or divorce coupon. This fee must accompany the application. Send check or money order payable to the Arkansas Department of Health. DO NOT SEND CASH. Of the total fee you send, $5.00 will be kept in this office to cover search charges for each record not found in our files.

FILL IN FOR A MARRIAGE RECORD

NAME OF GROOM _____

MAIDEN NAME OF BRIDE _____

DATE OF MARRIAGE _____
            Month   Day   Year

COUNTY IN WHICH LICENSE WAS ISSUED _____

FILL IN FOR A DIVORCE RECORD

NAME OF HUSBAND_____

NAME OF WIFE _____

DATE OF DIVORCE OR DISMISSAL _____
                    Month   Day   Year

COUNTY IN WHICH DIVORCE WAS GRANTED/DISMISSED _____

PLEASE ANSWER ALL QUESTIONS

What is your relationship to the parties named on the requested record?
_____

What is your reason for requesting a copy of this record?_____
_____

Signature and telephone number of person requesting this record:
_____

DO NOT WRITE IN THIS SPACE	
Searcher	
Index	
Volume No.	
Page No.	Yr.

DO NOT DETACH

THIS IS A MAILING INSERT. **PRINT** NAME AND ADDRESS OF PERSON TO WHOM THE CERTIFIED COPY IS TO BE MAILED.

THIS IS NOT AN INVOICE.

NO. OF COPIES REQUESTED
Marriage _____
Divorce _____
Amount of Money Enclosed _____

NAME _____

ADDRESS _____

CITY _____ STATE _____ ZIP _____

VR-9   A—3689

Any person who willfully and knowingly makes any false statement in an application for certified copy of a vital record filed in this state is subject to a fine of not more than ten thousand dollars ($10,000) or imprisoned not more than five (5) years, or both. (Ark. Statut 82-527).

DATE _____

ARKANSAS DEPARTMENT OF HEALTH
DIVISION OF VITAL RECORDS
4815 WEST MARKHAM STREET
LITTLE ROCK, ARKANSAS 72205-3867

APPLICATION FOR CERTIFIED COPY OF CERTIFICATE OF DEATH

Only Arkansas deaths are recorded in this office. There are no original death records for events which occurred before February 1, 1914. The fee is   for the first copy and   for each additional copy of the same record ordered at the same time. The fee must accompany the application. Send check or money order payable to the Arkansas Department of Health. DO NOT SEND CASH. Of the total fee you send, $4.00 will be kept in this office to cover search charges if no record of the death is found.

FULL NAME OF DECEASED _____
First   Middle   Last

DATE OF DEATH _____ AGE OF DECEASED _____ SEX _____ RACE _____

PLACE WHERE DEATH OCCURRED _____
City   County   State

If Unknown,
Give Last Place of Residence _____
City   County   State

NAME OF FUNERAL HOME _____

ADDRESS _____

NAME OF ATTENDING PHYSICIAN _____

ADDRESS _____

What is your relationship to the person whose certificate is being requested?
_____

What is your reason for requesting a copy of this record? _____
_____

If the death was not recorded, do you wish to file a delayed death record? _____

Signature and telephone number of person requesting this certificate:
_____

<table>
<tr><td colspan="2">DO NOT WRITE IN THIS SPACE</td></tr>
<tr><td colspan="2">Searcher</td></tr>
<tr><td colspan="2">Index</td></tr>
<tr><td>Delayed</td><td>Prior</td></tr>
<tr><td colspan="2">Volume No.</td></tr>
<tr><td>Page No.</td><td>Yr.</td></tr>
</table>

DO NOT DETACH

THIS IS A MAILING INSERT. PRINT NAME AND ADDRESS OF PERSON WHO IS TO RECEIVE THE COPY OR COPIES.

THIS IS NOT AN INVOICE

<table>
<tr><td colspan="2">COPIES REQUESTED</td></tr>
<tr><td></td><td>HOW MANY</td></tr>
<tr><td>ONE COPY
ADDITIONAL
COPIES</td><td>☐</td></tr>
<tr><td>AMOUNT
OF MONEY
ENCLOSED</td><td>$</td></tr>
</table>

NAME _____

ADDRESS _____

CITY _____ STATE _____ ZIP _____

VR-8

Ⓐ—3688

Any person who willfully and knowingly makes any false statement in an application for certified copy of a vital record filed in this state is subject to a fine of not more than ten thousand dollars ($10,000) or imprisoned not more than five (5) years, or both. (Ark. State 82-527).

CALIFORNIA

Send your requests to:

Office of the State Registrar of Vital Statistics
Department of Health Services
410 N Street
Sacramento, California 95814

(916) 445-2684

Cost for a certified Birth Certificate	$11.00
Cost for a certified Marriage Certificate	$11.00
Cost for a certified Death Certificate	$ 7.00

The Registrar has records from July 1, 1905.

APPLICATION FOR CERTIFIED COPY OF BIRTH RECORD

INFORMATION

Birth records have been maintained in the Office of the State Registrar of Vital Statistics since July 1, 1905. The only records of earlier events are delayed birth certificates and court order delayed birth certificates registered as provided by law.

INSTRUCTIONS

1. Use a separate application blank for each different record of birth for which you are requesting a certified copy. Send   for each certified copy requested. If no record of the birth is found, the   fee will be retained for searching as required by statute and a Certification of No Record will be sent.

2. Give all the information you have available for the identification of the record of the registrant in the spaces under registrant information. If the information you furnish is incomplete or inaccurate, it may be impossible to locate the record. If this person has been adopted, please make the request in the adopted name.

3. Complete the applicant information section.

4. Indicate the number of certified copies you wish and include with this application sufficient money in the form of a postal or bank money order (international money order only for out-of-country requests), made payable to the State Registrar of Vital Statistics; the fee is '_____ for each certified copy.

5. All copies are certified and have a raised state seal.

CERTIFICATE INFORMATION — PLEASE PRINT

Name on Certificate—First Name	Middle Name	Last Name or Birth Name If Married
City or Town of Birth		Place of Birth—County
Date of Birth—Month, Day, Year (If Unknown Enter Approximate Date of Birth)		Sex
Name of Father—First Name	Middle Name	Last Name
Birth Name of Mother—First Name	Middle Name	Last Name

APPLICANT INFORMATION — PLEASE PRINT

Purpose for Which Certified Copy Is to Be Used	Today's Date	Phone Number—Area Code First
Please Print—Name of Person Completing Application	Signature of Person Requesting Record/s—Your Signature ►	
Address—Street	City	State—Zip Code
Mailing Address for Copies If Different Than Above: Name	Number of Certified Copies Requested	Amount of Money Enclosed
Mailing Address—Street	City	State—Zip Code

DO NOT WRITE IN SPACES BELOW — FOR REGISTRAR

APPLICATION FOR CERTIFIED COPY OF MARRIAGE RECORD

INFORMATION

Marriage records have been maintained in the Office of the State Registrar of Vital Statistics since July 1, 1905.

INSTRUCTIONS

1. Use a separate application blank for each different record of marriage for which you are requesting a certified copy. Send for each certified copy requested. If no record of the marriage is found, the fee will be retained for searching as required by statute and a Certification of No Record will be sent.

2. Give all the information you have available for the identification of the record of marriage in the spaces under bride and groom information. If the information you furnish is incomplete or inaccurate, it may be impossible to locate the record.

3. Complete the applicant information section.

4. Indicate the number of certified copies you wish and include with this application sufficient money in the form of a postal or bank money order (International Money Order only for out-of-country requests), made payable to the State Registrar of Vital Statistics; the fee is for each certified copy. Enclose a self-addressed, stamped envelope to expedite filling your request.

5. All copies are certified and have a raised state seal.

FOR OFFICE USE ONLY

DATE	
CSU	
TCU	
IDU	
ARU	
SRU	
PHOTO	

BRIDE AND GROOM INFORMATION—PLEASE PRINT

Name of Groom — First Name	Middle Name	Last Name
Date of Birth	Place of Birth	Name of Father of Groom
Maiden Name of Bride—First Name	Middle Name	Last Name
Date of Birth	Place of Birth	Name of Father of Bride

Date of Marriage—Month, Day, Yr.	If Date Unknown, Enter Year(s) to be Searched	County of Issue of License	County of Marriage

APPLICANT INFORMATION—PLEASE TYPE OR PRINT

Enter Purpose for Which Certified Copy Is to be Used	Today's Date	Your Phone Number—Area Code First
Please Print—Name of Person Completing Application	Signature of Person Requesting Record/s—Your Signature	
Address—Street	City	State—Zip Code
Mailing Address For Copies If Different Than Above:	Number of Certified Copies Requested	Amount of Money Enclosed
Mailing Address—Street	City	State—Zip Code

DO NOT WRITE IN SPACES BELOW—FOR REGISTRAR

VS 113 (9/78)

66907-449 1-79 OSP 100M

APPLICATION FOR CERTIFIED COPY OF DEATH RECORD

FOR OFFICE USE ONLY

DATE	
CSU	
TCU	
IDU	
ARU	
SRU	
PHOTO	

INFORMATION

Death records have been maintained in the Office of the State Registrar of Vital Statistics since July 1, 1905.

INSTRUCTIONS

1. Use a separate application blank for each different record of death for which you are requesting a certified copy. Send   for each certified copy requested. If no record of the death is found, the   fee will be retained for searching as required by statute and a certificate of search will be sent.

2. Give all the information you have available for the identification of the record of the decedent in the spaces under decedent information. If the information you furnish is incomplete or inaccurate, it may be impossible to locate the record.

3. Complete the applicant information section.

4. Indicate the number of certified copies you wish and include with this application sufficient money in the form of a postal or bank money order (International Money Order only for out-of-country requests), made payable to the State Registrar of Vital Statistics; the fee is   for each certified copy.

5. All copies are certified and have a raised state seal.

DECEDENT INFORMATION—PLEASE PRINT

Name of Decedent—First Name	Middle Name	Last Name	Sex
Place of Death—City or Town	Place of Death—County	Place of Birth	Date of Birth—Month, Day, Year
Date of Death—Month, Day, Year—or Period of Years to be Searched		Social Security Number	
Mother's Maiden Name		Name of Spouse (Husband or Wife of Decedent)	

APPLICANT INFORMATION—PLEASE TYPE OR PRINT

Enter Purpose For Which Certified Copy is to be Used	Today's Date	Your Phone Number—Area Code First
Please Print—Name of Person Completing Application	Signature of Person Requesting Record/s—Your Signature	
Address—Street	City	State—Zip Code
Mailing Address For Copies if Different Than Above	Number of Certified Copies Requested	Amount of Money Enclosed
Mailing Address—Street	City	State—Zip Code

DO NOT WRITE IN SPACES BELOW—FOR REGISTRAR

COLORADO

Send your requests to:

Vital Records Section
Colorado Department of Health
4210 East 11th Avenue, Room 100
Denver, Colorado 80220

(303) 320-8474

Send your requests for Marriage Certificates to:

County Clerk
County Court House
(County where the Marriage License was issued)

Cost for a certified Birth Certificate	$6.00
Cost for a certified Death Certificate	$6.00

If you apply for a birth or death certificate in person and wait for the certificate to be prepared, the fee is $10.00. The Office requests that you include a self-addressed stamped envelope with your orders by mail. The Office has an index to marriage records from 1900 through 1939 and from 1975 through February 1985. The index gives the names of the persons married, date and county of the marriage. The fee is $2.00 to search the index. Contact the County Clerk for a copy of the marriage certificate.

If your request is urgent you may call and charge your certificates to your visa or mastercard. There is a $15.00 fee for this service. Call the Vital Records Section at (303) 331-4890 to arrange for this service.

APPLICATION FOR CERTIFIED COPY OF BIRTH CERTIFICATE
(This form must be completed IN FULL. PLEASE PRINT OR TYPE.)

Vital Records Section
Colorado Department of Health
4210 East 11th Avenue, Room 100
Denver, Colorado 80220

```
                             Fees
Regular Service:  Record mailed within 4 weeks or less.
          ☐           per copy or per search of files
                      if no record is found.
Priority Service: Record mailed within 5 days.
          ☐           per copy or per search of files
                      if no record is found.
          When date of birth is unknown, an additional    per
          year searched beyond one year is charged.
                      (no matter which service you choose)
Wallet Size:      (Contains limited information)
```

FULL name at birth _____
(If adopted, give new name)

Place of Birth _____   Date of Birth _____

Full name of father _____   Maiden name of mother _____

Purpose for
this copy: _____   YOUR
                                   SIGNATURE _____

These records are confidential. Please
state your relationship to child.   Street _____

PENALTY BY LAW if any person alters,   City _____   State _____   Zip _____
uses, attempts to use or furnishes
to another for deceptive use or   ( )
supplies false information for any   Your day time telephone number
vital statistics certificate.

If possible, please include a self-addressed, long envelope with your order.
Make your check or money order payable to Vital Records.

AD RS 2 (Rev. 7/87)   Number of copies ordered _____.   Amount enclosed $ _____.

APPLICATION FOR CERTIFIED COPY OF DEATH CERTIFICATE
(This form must be completed IN FULL.)

Vital Records Section
Colorado Department of Health
4210 East 11th Avenue, Room 100
Denver, Colorado 80220

	Fees
Regular Service: ☐	Record mailed within 4 weeks or less.
	per copy or per search of files
	if no record is found.
Priority Service: ☐	Record mailed within 5 days.
	per copy or per search of files
	if no record is found.
	When date of death is unknown, there is an an additional
	charge of per year searched beyond one year.

FULL Name of Deceased Person:
(At Time of Death)
_____

Place of Death _____ Date of Death _____

Purpose for this copy _____

These records are confidential. Please
state your relationship to the deceased: _____

If possible, please include a long,
self-addressed envelope with your order.

Your signature _____

Address _____
        Street

City _____ State _____ Zip _____

( ) _____
Your daytime telephone number

PENALTY BY LAW if any person alters,
uses, or attempts to use or furnishes
to another for deceptive use or
supplies false information for any
vital statistics certificate.

AD RS 1 (Rev. 3/87)

CONNECTICUT

Send your requests to:

Connecticut State Department of Health Services
Vital Records Unit
150 Washington Street
Hartford, Connecticut 06106

(203) 566-1124

Cost for a certified Birth Certificate	$3.00
Cost for a short form Birth Certificate	$2.00
Cost for a certified Marriage Certificate	$3.00
Cost for a certified Death Certificate	$3.00

The Connecticut State Department of Health Services has copies of vital records from July 1, 1897.

REQUEST FOR COPY OF BIRTH CERTIFICATE

VS-39B Rev. 174

Mail request with fee or bring to:
CONNECTICUT STATE DEPT. OF HEALTH

PLEASE PRINT.

I. BIRTH CERTIFICATE OF:

FULL NAME AT BIRTH

DATE OF BIRTH	SEX

PLACE OF BIRTH *(Town, Hospital)*

II. PARENTS OF PERSON NAMED IN BIRTH CERTIFICATE

FATHER'S FULL NAME	FATHER'S BIRTHPLACE *(Town)*
MOTHER'S FULL NAME	MOTHER'S BIRTHPLACE *(Town)*

RESIDENCE OF PARENTS AT TIME OF THIS BIRTH

TYPE OF COPY *(See explanations below)*	LEGAL FEE	NO. OF COPIES	AMOUNT ATTACHED
Full certified copy			$
Certification of birth			$

Full certified copy: Sufficient for all legal purposes. If requester is a minor (under 18 years of age), parent or guardian must sign this request.

Certification of birth: Wallet-size certificate; sufficient for Social Security, school, driver's license, and working papers.

III. PERSON MAKING THIS REQUEST

Your Name

Your Address

(No. and Street)

(Town, State)   *(Zip Code)*

▲ Your Signature

*For the protection of the individual, certificates of vital events are **not** open to public inspection.*

If the person making this request is not the person named in the certificate, *the following must be completed in order to permit this office to comply with the request.*

RELATIONSHIP TO PERSON NAMED IN CERTIFICATE *(e.g., parents, attorney)*	REASON FOR MAKING REQUEST

REQUEST FOR COPY OF MARRIAGE CERTIFICATE

VS-39M Rev. 1-74

Mail request with fee or bring to:

CONNECTICUT STATE DEPT. OF HEALTH

PLEASE PRINT.

| GROOM | FULL NAME *(First)* | *(Middle)* | *(Last)* |

| BRIDE | FULL NAME BEFORE MARRIAGE *(First)* | *(Middle)* | *(Last)* |

| DATE OF MARRIAGE *(Mo./Day/Year)* | PLACE OF MARRIAGE *(Town)* |

PERSON MAKING THIS REQUEST	YOUR NAME
	YOUR ADDRESS *(No. and Street)*
	(Town, State)	*(Zip Code)*

| NO. OF COPIES WANTED | AMOUNT ATTACHED $ |
| YOUR SIGNATURE |

For the protection of the individual, certificates of vital events are **not** *open to public inspection.*

If the person making this request is not the person named in the certificate, *the following must be completed in order to permit this office to comply with the request.*

| RELATIONSHIP TO PERSON NAMED IN CERTIFICATE *(e.g., attorney)* | REASON FOR MAKING REQUEST |

APPLICATION FOR DEATH CERTIFICATE

I am applying for the death certificate of :—

Full name .... Sex ....
.... (First name) .... (Family name)

Date of Death .... (or date last known to be alive)
.... (Month) .... (Day) .... (Year)

Place of death .... Date of birth ....
.... (Town) .... (Month) .... (Day) .... (Year)

Place of birth ....
.... (Town) .... (State or Foreign Country)

INFORMATION ON ABOVE PERSON'S FAMILY

Father's name .... Mother's name ....

If married, husband or wife's name ....

Signature and ....

address of person...

making application ....

CONNECTICUT STATE DEPARTMENT OF HEALTH
V.S. 39B (12-71) 2500

DELAWARE

Send your requests to:

Office of Vital Statistics
Division of Public Health
P.O. Box 637
Dover, Delaware 19903

(302) 736-4721

Cost for a certified Birth Certificate	$5.00
Cost for a certified Marriage Certificate	$5.00
Cost for a certified Death Certificate	$5.00
Cost for a duplicate copy, when ordered at the same time	$3.00

The Delaware Office of Vital Statistics has birth and death records from January 1, 1861 to December 31, 1863 and January 1, 1881 to the present. They hold marriage records from January 1, 1847.

If your request is urgent you may call and charge your certificates to your visa or mastercard. There is a $10.00 fee for this service.

RETURN TO. . . **OFFICE OF VITAL STATISTICS**
P.O. BOX 637
DOVER, DELAWARE   19903

Today's Date

Number of Copies

APPLICATION FOR BIRTH CERTIFICATE
COMPLETE ALL ITEMS REQUESTED BELOW AS ACCURATELY AS POSSIBLE

Full Name at Birth of Person Whose Record is Requested - If Name Has Ever Been Changed Please Give Details on Back

Date of Birth (Month, Day, Year)   *Place of Birth (Hospital)*

Full Maiden Name of Mother

Full Name of Father

If Known, Name of Doctor or Midwife

For What Purpose is Certificate Needed

PLEASE COMPLETE
YOUR NAME AND
MAILING ADDRESS

NAME _____

STREET ADDRESS _____

TOWN _____ STATE _____

ZIP CODE _____

**OFFICE OF VITAL STATISTICS
P.O. BOX 637
DOVER, DELAWARE   19903**

APPLICATION FOR A MARRIAGE CERTIFICATE

COMPLETE ALL ITEMS REQUESTED BELOW AS ACCURATELY AS POSSIBLE

_____

FULL NAME OF GROOM _____

FULL MAIDEN NAME OF BRIDE_____

PLACE OF MARRIAGE_____

DATE OF MARRIAGE_____

NAME OF OFFICIATING MINISTER_____

★★★★

MAIL COPY TO ....NAME_____

STREET ADDRESS_____

TOWN_____

STATE_____ZIP _____
                                  CODE

_____

APPLICATION FOR A CERTIFIED COPY OF A DEATH CERTIFICATE

(Complete items requested below accurately as possible)

===

Name of decedent _____ Race _____

Date of decease _____ Place of decease _____

Full name of decedent's father _____ Full maiden name of mother _____

For what purpose is certificate needed _____

_____

SEND COPY TO . . . . .   _____
Name

_____
Street/Development/Rural Delivery/Box Number

_____
City/Town   State   Zip Code

===

If the record is not found the fee will be retained for the search

Insufficient fee being returned _____

If a check with the incorrect fee is being returned do not alter. Make another check.

DISTRICT OF COLUMBIA

Send your requests to:

Vital Records Branch
Government of the District of Columbia
Department of Human Services
425 I Street N.W., Room 3007
Washington, DC 20001

(202) 727-5314

Send your requests for Marriage Certificates to:

Marriage Bureau
Superior Court of the District of Columbia
515 5th Street, N.W., Room 111
Washington, DC 20001

(202) 879-2839

Cost for a certified Birth Certificate	$5.00
Cost for a certified Marriage Certificate	$5.00
Cost for a certified Death Certificate	$5.00

The Vital Records Branch has birth and death records from January 1, 1874. Marriage records are available from January 1, 1982 and must be ordered from the Superior Court.

GOVERNMENT OF THE DISTRICT OF COLUMBIA
DEPARTMENT OF HUMAN SERVICES

RETURN OF CORRESPONDENCE

The attached request is being returned for the following reason(s):

[ ] The information given is insufficient for a thorough search. Please complete the form below and return to this office:

Vital Records Branch
425 I Street, N. W.
Room 3007
Washington, D. C. 20001

[ ] The District of Columbia registers only births/deaths that occur in the District of Columbia. Please see the reverse side of this form for your state's address.

[ ] NO RECORDS REGISTERED PRIOR TO 1874

[ ] <u>APPLICATION FOR CERTIFIED COPY OF BIRTH CERTIFICATE(S)</u> [Please Print]
     Choice of Certificate: [ ] Wallet & Long Form (computer)
                             [ ] Complete Copy (xerox or microfilm)
                             Note: <u>either are legal records</u>

Name at Birth:_____
              (First)   (Middle)   (Last)

Date of Birth_____ Place of Birth (DC)_____   Sex_____

Father's Name_____ Mother's Maiden Name_____

Purpose:_____ Relationship:_____

Signature:_____

Mailing Address:_____

DHS-13 (Rev. 3/84)

[ ] <u>APPLICATION FOR CERTIFIED COPY OF DEATH CERTIFICATE(S)</u> [Please Print]

Full Name of Deceased:_____Race:(optional)_____

Date of Death:_____ Place of Death in DC:_____

If Date of Death not known, then date last known alive:_____ _____

Age at Time   Name of   Name of
of Death:_____ Spouse:_____ Father:_____

Last known address of deceased:_____

Name of Funeral Director:_____

Requester's Signature:_____

Mailing Address:_____

DHS-14 (Rev. 3/84)

WARNING: Vital Records are not public records. Vital Records may be issued only to the registrant, members of his/her family, or persons acting on behalf of the registrant or his/her estate.

FLORIDA

Send your requests to:

> State of Florida
> Department of Health and Rehabilitation Services
> Vital Statistics
> P.O. Box 210
> Jacksonville, Florida 32231-0042

(904) 359-6900

Cost for a certified Birth Certificate	$7.00
Cost for a certified Marriage Certificate	$3.00
Cost for a certified Death Certificate	$3.00
Cost for a duplicate copy, when ordered at the same time	$2.00

The first State law requiring registration was passed in 1899. However, the Office of Vital Statistics has birth records from April 1865 and death records from August 1877 to the present. The Office has marriage records from June 6, 1927 to date.

If your request is urgent you may call and charge your certificates to your visa or mastercard. There is a $4.25 fee for this service.

PLEASE TYPE OR PRINT CLEARLY

HRS APPLICATION FOR BIRTH RECORD FOR PERSON BORN IN FLORIDA

(IMPORTANT - Read information and instructions on other side before completing this form)

FULL NAME AT BIRTH	First	Middle	Last
BIRTH NUMBER (if known)			Age
DATE OF BIRTH	Month	Day	Year
			Sex
PLACE OF BIRTH	Hospital	City	County
			FLORIDA
FATHER'S NAME	First	Middle	Last
MOTHER'S MAIDEN NAME (Name before marriage)	First	Middle	Last (maiden)

NO REFUNDS (except fees for duplicate copies where no record is located)

Number ordered _____ $ _____

LONG FORM CERTIFICATION: Issued to parent, guardian, person named on birth record (if 18 years old), legal representative, certain official agencies, or upon court order (applicants not entitled to long form will automatically be sent a short form).

WALLET SIZE PLASTIC CARD: Same data as short form. .... $ _____

MINIMUM PROCESSING CHARGE PER ORDER .... $ _____

EXPEDITED PROCESSING (OPTIONAL): Guaranteed mailing of order by day after receipt of payment. .... $ _____

TOTAL ENCLOSED: (Check ☐ Money order ☐) Cash accepted at Vital Records office window - DO NOT MAIL CASH. Make check or money order payable to Vital Statistics. Florida Law imposes a service charge of $10.00 in addition to other penalties for dishonored checks. .... $ _____

APPLICANT'S SIGNATURE	
RELATIONSHIP TO PERSON NAMED ON CERTIFICATE IF ATTORNEY, **NAME PERSON YOU REPRESENT**	IF BIRTH RECORDS ARE TO BE MAILED TO DIFFERENT ADDRESS, MAIL TO:
	NUMBER / STREET
ADDRESS: CITY	STATE / ZIP

HRS Form 726, Oct 85 (Obsoletes previous editions as of 9/30/85)
(Stock Number: 5740-000-0726-8)

APPLICATION FOR MARRIAGE RECORD

(For Marriage Licenses Issued in Florida)

PLEASE TYPE OR PRINT CLEARLY:

		Race or Color
NAME OF GROOM		
NAME OF BRIDE		Race or Color
DATE OF MARRIAGE		If exact date is unknown, indicate which years are to be searched.
PLACE LICENSE ISSUED	FLORIDA	Give **county (or city)** in which license was obtained.

ENCLOSED FIND REMITTANCE (Check ☐ Money Order ☐ Cash ☐)
(Please make check or money order payable to State of Florida,
Vital Statistics.) —**NO REFUNDS—**

NOTE: Send cash at your own risk $_____
We are not responsible for cash lost in the mail.
$10.00 **SERVICE FEE** must be paid on all
dishonored checks, drafts or money orders.
This is in addition to all other penalties imposed
by law. Florida Statutes 832.07 (1)(a).

APPLICANT'S SIGNATURE	Signed		
ADDRESS	Number	Street	MAILING ADDRESS FOR COPIES IF DIFFERENT FROM APPLICANT'S
	City	State	

AVAILABILITY OF RECORDS: Marriage records for Florida were centralized in the Office of Vital Statistics on June 6, 1927 and certified copies of these records may be obtained upon request. For marriage records prior to that date, write to the County Judge of the county in which the license was issued. Copies of the 'Application for Marriage' processed prior to 1972 must also be obtained from the issuing County Judge.

HRS Form 261, Jul 84 (Replaces Jul 83 edition which may be used)
(Stock Number: 5740-000-0261-4)

APPLICATION FOR DEATH RECORD

(For Death which occurred in Florida)

PLEASE TYPE OR PRINT CLEARLY

NAME c. DECEASED				Race	Sex
DATE OF DEATH	Month and Day	Year		If exact date unknown give approximate date	
PLACE OF DEATH	City	County	FLORIDA		
NAME OF FUNERAL DIRECTOR					

AVAILABILITY OF RECORDS: The first State Law requiring the registration of deaths was enacted in 1899. However, there are some records on file dating back to 1877.

ENCLOSED FIND REMITTANCE (Check ☐ Money Order ☐ Cash ☐)
(Please make check or money order payable to State of Florida, Vital Statistics.)

NOTE: Send cash at your own risk $_____ We are not responsible for cash lost in the mail. $10.00 SERVICE FEE must be paid on all dishonored checks, drafts or money orders. This is in addition to all other penalties imposed by law. Florida Statutes 832.07 (1)(a).

PLEASE PROVIDE THE FOLLOWING: A. Certified Photostat Copy .... Number Desired _____

B. Expedited Processing .... Yes ☐ No ☐
(check correct box)

APPLICANTS SIGNATURE	Signed	MAILING ADDRESS FOR COPIES IF DIFFERENT FROM APPLICANT'S
RELATIONSHIP TO DECEASED		
ADDRESS:	Number	Street
	City	State	ZIP

HRS Form 727, Jul 83 (Obsoletes previous editions)
(Stock Number: 5740-000-0727-6)

GEORGIA

Send your requests to:

Georgia Department of Human Resources
Vital Records Unit
Room 217-H, Health Building
47 Trinity Avenue, S.W.
Atlanta, Georgia 30334

(404) 656-4750

Cost for a certified Birth Certificate	$3.00
Cost for a certified Birth Card	$4.00
Cost for an additional copy of Birth Card	$2.00
Cost for a certified Marriage Certificate	$3.00
Cost for a certified Death Certificate	$3.00
Cost for a duplicate copy, when ordered at the same time	$1.00

The Georgia Department of Human Resources has birth and death records from January 1, 1919 to the present. They also hold marriage records from June 9, 1952 to the present. The Department requires payment in the form of a U.S. postal money order, cashier's check, or certified check.

If your request is urgent you may call and charge your certificates to your visa or mastercard. There is a $22.00 fee for this service, which includes the postal costs.

Georgia Department of Human Resources
VITAL RECORDS SERVICE
Room 217-H, 47 Trinity Ave., S.W.
Atlanta, Georgia 30334

REQUEST FOR SEARCH OF VITAL RECORDS — GEORGIA CERTIFICATES ONLY

THIS SPACE FOR OFFICE USE ONLY

FILL IN INFORMATION BELOW CONCERNING PERSON WHOSE CERTIFICATE IS REQUESTED —
PLEASE FOLLOW THE NUMBERS AND PRINT ALL INFORMATION.

Certificate Number

Years Searched

Clerk's Initials

1 CHECK THE TYPE OF CERTIFICATE REQUESTED: *(ONE Request Form Per Certificate)*

☐ BIRTH ☐ DEATH ☐ MARRIAGE ☐ DIVORCE ☐ OTHER

(1919 To Present)   (1952 To Present)

2 ENTER THE NUMBER OF CERTIFIED COPIES REQUESTED:

☐ FULL Certified Copy of Certificate   ☐ Birth Registration Card (Wallet Size)   ☐ Total Number of Copies Requested

NOTE:
IF DELAYED CERTIFICATE OF BIRTH WAS PREVIOUSLY FILED, GIVE DATE _____

Amount Received
$ _____
Search Fee

$ _____
Amendment Fee

$ _____
Filing Fee, Delayed

$ _____
Replacement Fee

$ _____
Total Fees

$ _____
Refund (if any)

$ _____

3 Name on Certificate   4 Date of Event

5 Age   6 Race   7 Sex   8 Place of Event   (County)   (State)

9 Full Name of Father (if this is a Marriage or Divorce Request, enter spouse's name here)

10 Full Name of Mother (include maiden name)

11 _____
(Signature of Requester)

MACHINE VALIDATION

MACHINE VALIDATION

NOTE:
Fill in only the MAIL TO: information below.
This label will be used to mail your certificate to you.
PLEASE PRINT NAME AND ADDRESS CORRECTLY AND LEGIBLY.

Address Correspondence to:
Georgia Department of Human Resources
VITAL RECORDS SERVICE
Room 217-H, 47 Trinity Ave., S.W.
Atlanta, Georgia 30334

OFFICE USE ONLY

NAME ON CERTIFICATE _____
DATE OF EVENT _____

Certificate Number

☐ Copy(ies) Issued
☐ Search Fee
☐ Voucher
☐ Refund

Amount Refunded $ _____

MAIL TO:

_____
_____
_____

Form 3918 (Rev. 12-82)

Georgia Department of Human Resources
Vital Records Unit
Room 217—H, Health Building, 47 Trinity Avenue, S.W.
Atlanta, Georgia 30334
REQUEST FOR SEARCH OF DEATH RECORDS

FOR OFFICE USE ONLY
Certificate Number_____
Years Searched_____
Clerk's Initials_____

PLEASE INDICATE BELOW THE NUMBER OF COPIES NEEDED AND FORWARD THIS FORM WITH EITHER A MONEY ORDER OR CHECK FOR THE CORRECT AMOUNT MADE PAYABLE TO THE GEORGIA DEPARTMENT OF HUMAN RESOURCES.

Total Number of Copies   Amount Received $ _____

FILL IN INFORMATION BELOW CONCERNING PERSON WHOSE CERTIFICATE IS REQUESTED

Name_____Date of Death _____
    (First)   (Middle)   (Last)

Age_____Race_____Sex _____Place of Death _____
    (Hospital)   (City)   (County)   (State)

If Married, Name of Husband or Wife _____

Occupation of Deceased _____ Funeral Director's Name _____

Name of Doctor_____Place of Burial _____
    (City)   (County)   (State)

List below name and address of person to whom certificate is to be mailed.

FOR OFFICE USE ONLY
☐ C.C. Issued   ☐ Refund
☐ Search Fee   Refunded
☐ Voucher   Amount_____

Name _____

Address _____
    (No. & Street or RFD and Box No.)   (Apt. No.)

_____
    (City)   (State)   (Zip Code)

MACHINE VALIDATION

OAS(5)—17 (Rev. 9-74)   DO NOT WRITE IN SPACE BELOW

Georgia Department of Human Resources
Vital Records Unit
Room 217—H, Health Building, 47 Trinity Avenue, S.W.
Atlanta, Georgia 30334

Name
DOD

MACHINE VALIDATION

Death Certificate Number

☐ C.C. Issued   ☐ Refund
☐ Search Fee   Refunded
☐ Voucher   Amount _____

OAS(5)—17 (Rev. 9-74)

HAWAII

State Department of Health
Research and Statistics Office
Vital Records Section
P.O. Box 3378
Honolulu, Hawaii 96801

(808) 548-5819

Cost for a certified Birth Certificate	$2.00
Cost for a certified Marriage Certificate	$2.00
Cost for a certified Death Certificate	$2.00

The Hawaii Vital Records Section has birth, marriage, and death records from the mid-nineteenth century.

STATE OF HAWAII, DEPARTMENT OF HEALTH
RESEARCH AND STATISTICS OFFICE

REQUEST FOR CERTIFIED COPY OF **BIRTH** RECORD

	FIRST	MIDDLE	LAST
NAME ON CERTIFICATE			

	MONTH	DAY	YEAR		CITY OR TOWN	ISLAND
DATE OF BIRTH:				PLACE OF BIRTH:		

	FIRST	MIDDLE	LAST
FATHER'S NAME:			

	FIRST	MIDDLE	MAIDEN NAME
MOTHER'S NAME:			

NUMBER OF COPIES _____	AMOUNT ATTACHED $ _____

ALL ITEMS MUST BE COMPLETED IN FULL TO PERMIT THIS OFFICE TO COMPLY WITH THIS REQUEST. FOR THE PROTECTION OF THE INDIVIDUAL, CERTIFICATES OF VITAL EVENTS ARE NOT OPEN TO PUBLIC INSPECTION.

RELATIONSHIP OF REQUESTOR TO PERSON NAMED ON CERTIFICATE

REASON FOR REQUESTING A CERTIFIED COPY

SIGNATURE OF REQUESTOR:	TELEPHONE NUMBERS
	RES.:
PRINT OR TYPE NAME OF REQUESTOR:	BUS.:

MAIL TO:
NAME	
NO. AND STREET OR P. O. BOX	
CITY	STATE	ZIP

FOR OFFICE USE ONLY		
Index Searched	Volumes Searched	Date Copy Prepared
From To	From To	
Year	Volume	Certificate	Receipt Number

RS 135 (Rev. 1/84)

REQUEST FOR COPY OF **MARRIAGE** OR **DIVORCE** RECORD

	MARRIAGE	DIVORCE
AMOUNT ATTACHED $ _____	NO. OF COPIES _____	NO. OF COPIES _____

	FIRST	MIDDLE	LAST
GROOM'S NAME:			

	FIRST	MIDDLE	LAST
BRIDE'S NAME:			

		MONTH	DAY	YEAR
DATE OF	MARRIAGE: OR DIVORCE:			

		CITY OR TOWN	ISLAND
PLACE OF	MARRIAGE: OR DIVORCE		

ALL ITEMS MUST BE COMPLETED IN FULL TO PERMIT THIS OFFICE TO COMPLY WITH THIS REQUEST. FOR THE PROTECTION OF THE INDIVIDUAL, CERTIFICATES OF VITAL EVENTS ARE NOT OPEN TO PUBLIC INSPECTION.

RELATIONSHIP OF REQUESTOR TO PERSONS NAMED ON CERTIFICATE

REASON FOR REQUESTING A CERTIFIED COPY

	TELEPHONE NUMBERS
SIGNATURE OF REQUESTOR:	RES.:
PRINT OR TYPE NAME OF REQUESTOR:	BUS.:

MAIL TO:
NAME	
NO. AND STREET OR P. O. BOX	
CITY	STATE	ZIP

FOR OFFICE USE ONLY		
Index Searched	Volumes Searched	Date Copy Prepared
From To	From To	
Year	Volume	Certificate	Receipt Number

RS 137 (Rev. 1/84)

STATE OF HAWAII, DEPARTMENT OF HEALTH
RESEARCH AND STATISTICS OFFICE

REQUEST FOR CERTIFIED COPY OF **DEATH** RECORD

AMOUNT
ATTACHED $ ....

NUMBER OF COPIES
REQUESTED: ....

	FIRST	MIDDLE	LAST
NAME OF DECEASED:			

	MONTH	DAY	YEAR
DATE OF DEATH:			

	CITY OR TOWN	ISLAND
PLACE OF DEATH:		

ALL ITEMS MUST BE COMPLETED IN FULL TO PERMIT THIS OFFICE TO COMPLY WITH THIS REQUEST. FOR THE PROTECTION OF THE INDIVIDUAL, CERTIFICATES OF VITAL EVENTS ARE NOT OPEN TO PUBLIC INSPECTION.

RELATIONSHIP OF REQUESTOR TO DECEASED

REASON FOR REQUESTING A CERTIFIED COPY

	TELEPHONE NUMBERS
SIGNATURE OF REQUESTOR:	RES.:
PRINT OR TYPE NAME OF REQUESTOR:	BUS.:

MAIL TO:

NAME

NO. AND STREET OR P. O. BOX

CITY   STATE   ZIP

FOR OFFICE USE ONLY		
Index Searched	Volumes Searched	Date Copy Prepared
From To	From To	
Year	Volume	Certificate	Receipt Number

RS 136 (Rev. 1/84)

IDAHO

Send your requests to:

State of Idaho
Department of Health and Welfare
Bureau of Vital Statistics
(450 West State Street)
State House
Boise, Idaho 83720

(208) 334-5980

Cost for a certified Birth Certificate	$6.00
Cost for a plastic Birth Certificate	$6.00
Cost for a certified Marriage Certificate	$6.00
Cost for a certified Death Certificate	$6.00

The Idaho State Office of Vital Statistics has birth and death records from July 1911 and marriage records from May 1947.

BIRTH CERTIFICATE APPLICATION
(For Persons Born in Idaho)

MAIL TO: **VITAL STATISTICS**
450 W. State Street
Boise, ID 83720

Name on Certificate _____
              (First)   *(Middle)*   *(Last)*

Place of Birth _____ File Number _____
         (City)   *(County)*   *(If Known)*

If Home Birth Give Exact Address _____

Date of Birth _____ Sex _____
         (Month)   *(Day)*   *(Year)*

Father's Name _____

Mother's Maiden Name _____

Purpose _____   Circle if Applicable: a. RUSH
                                                       b. Twin Birth

Signature of Applicant _____

Address _____
     (Street)   *(City)*   *(State)*   *(Zip)*

Relationship _____

Number of Copies Requested: Certified Copy _____ Plastic Wallet Card _____

PLEASE COMPLETE THE FOLLOWING IF THE CERTIFICATE IS TO BE MAILED
(Please Print Clearly)

_____
Name

_____
Street

_____
City   State   Zip   HWH 0160

APPLICATION FOR A MARRIAGE CERTIFICATE

Address correspondence and make money order payable to:

BUREAU OF VITAL STATISTICS, STANDARDS AND LOCAL HEALTH SERVICES
Department of Health and Welfare

Boise, Idaho   83720

FULL NAME OF GROOM _____

FULL NAME OF BRIDE _____

DATE OF MARRIAGE _____

CITY OF LICENSE APPLICATION _____

SIGNATURE OF APPLICANT _____

ADDRESS _____

RELATIONSHIP TO ABOVE PERSONS _____

Number of certified copies requested: _____
The fee for each certified copy and/or search is

NOTE: *Marriages have been filed with the State office since May, 1947. Prior to that time, they are filed with the County Recorder of each County in the State.*

HW-0161

APPLICATION FOR AN IDAHO DEATH CERTIFICATE

Note: Death records have been filed in Idaho since July 1911.

ADDRESS CORRESPONDENCE AND MAKE MONEY ORDER PAYABLE TO:

VITAL STATISTICS
450 W. State Street
Boise, ID   83720

1. Full name of deceased at death _____

2. Place of death _____ (City/Town) _____ (County)

3. Date of death _____ (Month/Day/Year)   (If unknown, need approximate year or range to search)

4. Signature of applicant _____

    Address _____

    Relationship to person named in item #1 _____

Number of certified copies requested: _____ The fee for each certified copy and/or search is

FOR DEATHS PRIOR TO 1969 PLEASE COMPLETE THE FOLLOWING: Purpose _____

Birth Date _____ (Month/Day/Year)   Birth Place _____ (City/State)   Spouse _____

Mother's Maiden Name _____   Father's Name _____

ILLINOIS

Send your requests to:

Illinois Department of Public Health
Division of Vital Records
605 West Jefferson Street
Springfield, Illinois 62761

(217) 782-6553

Send your requests for Marriage Certificates to:

Clerk
Superior Court
(County where the Marriage License was issued)

Cost for a certified Birth Certificate	$15.00
Cost for a short form Birth Certificate	$10.00
Cost for a certified Birth Card	$10.00
Cost for an uncertified record	$10.00
Cost for a verified Marriage Certificate	$ 5.00
Cost for a certified Death Certificate	$15.00
Cost for a duplicate copy, when ordered at the same time	$ 2.00

The Illinois Department of Public Health has birth and death records from January 1, 1916. They hold marriage records from January 1, 1962.

If your request is urgent you may call and charge your certificates to your visa or mastercard. There is a $29.75 fee for this, which includes the postal charges.

APPLICATION FOR SEARCH OF BIRTH RECORD FILES
(Furnish all possible information-TYPE OR PRINT)

FULL NAME:	First	Middle	Last

PLACE OF BIRTH:	Street, RFD., Hosp.	City or Town	County

DATE OF BIRTH:	Month	Day	Year	SEX:	BIRTH NUMBER IF KNOWN:

FATHER:

MOTHER:	Maiden Name	Married Name

CERTIFIED COPY	CERTIFICATION	BIRTH CARD (Wallet Size)
Amount Enclosed: $_____	Amount Enclosed: $_____	Amount Enclosed: $_____
For _____ copies	For _____ copies	For _____ copies

Application Made By: | **Mail Copy to (if other than applicant):**

NAME: (written signature)

NAME:

STREET ADDRESS:

STREET ADDRESS:

CITY:	STATE:	ZIP

CITY:	STATE:	ZIP

YOUR RELATIONSHIP TO PERSON:

INTENDED USE OF DOCUMENT:

NOTE: Birth certificates are confidential records, and copies can be issued only to persons entitled to receive them. The application must indicate the requestor's relationship to the person and the intended use of the document.

CERTIFICATION

Local File Number   STATE OF ILLINOIS   State File Number
Certification of Birth Record   112-

Name _____ Sex _____
Place of birth _____ County _____
Date of birth _____ , 19 _____
Record amended on _____ , 19 _____

I HEREBY CERTIFY that the above information was taken from the birth record of the person named, which was filed in my office in accordance with Illinois statutes, and that this certification is issued in accordance with those statutes.

Signed _____ Date _____ , 19 _____
Title _____ Address _____
VR-183 (10/70r)

CERTIFIED COPY

STATE OF ILLINOIS
CERTIFICATE OF LIVE BIRTH   112-

VR 180 (1/84r)-DIV. OF VITAL RECORDS-ILLINOIS DEPT. OF PUBLIC HEALTH-SPRINGFIELD, IL. 62761

APPLICATION FOR SEARCH OF DEATH RECORD FILES

(Furnish all possible information–TYPE OR PRINT)

FULL NAME OF DECEASED:	First	Middle	Last

PLACE OF DEATH:	Hospital	City or Town	County

DATE OF DEATH:	Month Day Year	SEX:	RACE:	OCCUPATION:

DATE LAST KNOWN TO BE ALIVE:	Month Day Year	LAST KNOWN ADDRESS:	MARITAL STATUS:

DATE OF BIRTH:	Month Day Year	BIRTHPLACE: (City and State)	NAME OF HUSBAND OR WIFE:

FULL NAME OF FATHER OF DECEASED:	FULL MAIDEN NAME OF MOTHER OF DECEASED:

CERTIFIED COPY	CERTIFICATION	GENEALOGICAL RESEARCH
Amount Enclosed:$ _____ for _____ copies	Amount Enclosed:$ _____ for _____ copies	Amount Enclosed:$ _____ for _____ year search

(DO NOT SEND CASH) Make check of money order payable to: Illinois Department of Public Health.

* A CERTIFICATION shows only the name of deceased, sex, place of death, date of death, date filed, and certificate number.

* A FULL CERTIFIED COPY is an exact photographic copy of the original death certificate.

Please indicate above the type and number of copies requested and return this form with the proper fee.

APPLICATION MADE BY:	MAIL COPY TO: (if other than applicant)
NAME:	NAME:
FIRM NAME: (if any)	FIRM NAME: (if any)
STREET ADDRESS:	STREET ADDRESS:
CITY: STATE: ZIP:	CITY: STATE: ZIP:

VR 280 (1/84R) DIV. OF VITAL RECORDS,ILLINOIS DEPT. OF PUBLIC HEALTH,SPRINGFIELD, IL. 62761

Send your requests to:

Indiana State Board of Health
1330 West Michigan Street
P.O. Box 1964
Indianapolis, Indiana 46206

(317) 633-0276

Send your requests for Marriage Certificates to:

Clerk of the Court
(County where the Marriage License was issued)

Cost for a certified Birth Certificate	$6.00
Cost for a certified Death Certificate	$4.00
Cost for a duplicate copy, when ordered at the same time	$1.00

The Indiana State Board of Health has birth records from October 1907 and death records from January 1900. While marriage records are only in the courts in each county, the State does have an index to marriages from January 1958 to the present. The Board of Health, at this time, only issues an application form for birth certificates.

 **STATE** of **INDIANA**  **INDIANAPOLIS**

STATE BOARD OF HEALTH

AN EQUAL OPPORTUNITY EMPLOYER

Address Reply to:
Indiana State Board of Health
1330 West Michigan Street
P. O. Box 1964
Indianapolis, IN 46206

MR# _____ Date Rec'd _____

☐ Your fee of $_____ was received
and is being held pending return of information
requested below.

☐ Please remit additional fee of
$ _____

Application for Search and Certified Copy of Birth Record. Please Complete All Items Below.

Full Name at Birth _____

Could this birth be recorded under any other name? If so, please give name:

_____

Has this Person Ever Been Adopted? Yes _____ No _____ If YES, please give name **AFTER** adoption

_____

Place of Birth: City _____ County _____

Date of Birth: _____ Age Last Birthday _____

Full Name of Father: _____ _____
(If adopted, give name of adoptive father)

Full Name of Mother Before Marriage: _____
(If adopted, give name of adoptive mother)

Purpose For Which Record Is To Be Used: _____

Your Relationship to person whose birth record is requested _____

FOR STATE OFFICE USE

Vol. _____
Cert. # _____
Filed _____
Am. Date _____
S. Clerk _____
_____

Total Certificates _____ Total Fee $ _____

Signature of Applicant _____

Mailing Address _____

City and State _____ Zip _____

Original birth records filed with this office begin October 1907. If birth occurred before this date, contact the
health officer in the county where the birth occurred.

SBH06-040 2/79
State Form 35485

VR-12

IOWA

Send your requests to:

Iowa State Department of Health
Vital Records Section
Lucas State Office Building
Des Moines, Iowa 50319

(515) 281-4944

Cost for a certified Birth Certificate	$6.00
Cost for a certified Marriage Certificate	$6.00
Cost for a certified Death Certificate	$6.00
Cost for a duplicate copy, when ordered at the same time	$6.00

The Iowa State Department of Health has records from July 1, 1880 to the present. However, the State did not make registration mandatory until July 1921, consequently less than 50% of the vital records were recorded before that date.

If your request is urgent you may call and charge your certificates to your visa or mastercard. There is a $5.00 fee for this service.

IOWA STATE DEPARTMENT OF HEALTH
VITAL RECORDS SECTION
LUCAS STATE OFFICE BLDG.
DES MOINES, IOWA 50319

THIS IS AN APPLICATION FOR CERTIFIED COPY OF RECORD OF:

BIRTH ☐

(Please check ONLY one) DEATH ☐

MARRIAGE ☐

1. Name on Record _____
   (If marriage record application, please provide both bride's and groom's names and county in which license was applied for).

   _____

2. Date of Event _____

3. City and/or County of Event _____

4. Father's Name _____
   (Please complete ONLY if this is a birth or death record application).

5. Mother's Maiden Name _____
   (Please complete ONLY if this is a birth or death record application).

6. Purpose for this copy _____

7. Has a copy of this record ever been received from this office? _____

8. Has name on certificate applied for ever been changed by court procedure? If so, please provide the name change _____

9. If this is a birth record application, is this the first-born child of this mother?___
   or the ___2nd? ___3rd? ___4th? ___5th?

(When mailing in an application, please enclose a stamped, self-addressed envelope).

Applicant's Signature _____

Applicant's Relationship _____ Tel.No. _____

NO ORIGINAL RECORDS ARE ON FILE IN THIS OFFICE PRIOR TO JULY 1, 1880.

NAME AND ADDRESS:

_____ PICKUP ☐

_____

_____ MAIL ☐

220-0225 (6/85)
CPE-69365

KANSAS

Send your requests to:

Kansas State Department of Health and Environment
Office of Vital Statistics
900 S.W. Jackson
Topeka, Kansas 66612-1290

(913) 296-1400

Cost for a certified Birth Certificate	$6.00
Cost for a wallet size Birth Certificate	$6.00
Cost for a certified Marriage Certificate	$6.00
Cost for a certified Death Certificate	$6.00
Cost for a duplicate copy, when ordered at the same time	$3.00

The Kansas Office of Vital Statistics has birth and death records from July 1, 1911. They hold marriage records from May 1, 1913.

If your request is urgent you may call and charge your certificates to your visa or mastercard. There is a $5.00 fee for this service.

KANSAS STATE DEPARTMENT OF HEALTH AND ENVIRONMENT
VITAL STATISTICS

APPLICATION FOR CERTIFIED COPY OF BIRTH CERTIFICATE

INSTRUCTIONS: Provisions of K.A.R. 28-17-6 require a fee of _____ for the first certified copy of a birth certificate and _____ for each additional copy of the same certificate requested at the same time. The certified copy fee must accompany this request. Make check payable to State Registrar of Vital Statistics. Cash sent by mail will be at applicant's risk.

If no birth record is located, the form and instructions for filing a Delayed Birth Certificate will be sent. The fee will be temporarily retained and may be applied to the cost of filing a delayed certificate. Fees expire 12 months from date paid.

FACTS CONCERNING THIS BIRTH

Full name on certificate _____

Date of birth _____ Present age of this person _____
    (Month)   (Day)   (Year)

Place of birth _____ Sex _____
    (City)   (County)   (State)

Full name of father _____ Birthplace _____

Full maiden name of mother _____ Birthplace _____

Is this birth certificate for an adopted child? _____ Legal change of name, other than by marriage? _____
If so, state original name (if known) _____

NOTICE: It is a violation of State and Federal Laws for anyone to make, sell or offer for sale any birth record for false identification purposes.

I hereby declare that as the applicant for a certified copy of the above described certificate, I have direct interest in the matter recorded and that the information therein contained is necessary for determination of personal or property rights, as per K.S.A. 65-2422(c).

Signature of person making request _____ Date of request _____

Relationship to person whose certificate is requested _____

PLEASE ENCLOSE SELF-ADDRESSED STAMPED ENVELOPE

PLEASE PRINT CORRECT MAILING ADDRESS:

_____
(Name)

_____
(Street Address)

_____
(City)   (State)   (Zip)

COPIES REQUESTED:

	Number
Complete Copy.....................	
Wallet Size Card	
(Not including Parents)	

REASON FOR REQUEST:

Social Security .... (_____)
Passport............................ (_____)
Genealogy .... (_____)
Other (School, Drivers License, etc.) ... (_____)

Total fee enclosed .. $ _____

Form VS-235 Rev. 7-1983

KANSAS STATE DEPARTMENT OF HEALTH AND ENVIRONMENT

Vital Statistics

APPLICATION FOR CERTIFIED COPY OF MARRIAGE LICENSE

Marriage records are on file from May 1, 1913. Provisions of K.A.R. 28-17-6 require a fee of _____ for the first certified copy of a marriage record and _____ for each additional copy of the same record ordered at the same time. Check or money order should be made payable to the State Registrar of Vital Statistics. Cash sent by mail will be at applicant's risk.

_____

FACTS CONCERNING THIS MARRIAGE

Name of groom_____ Age at time of marriage_____

Maiden name of bride_____ Age at time of marriage_____

Date of marriage_____ _____

County in which marriage license was issued_____

City or town in which marriage took place_____

Notice: It is a violation of State and Federal Laws for anyone to make, sell, or offer for sale, any marriage record for false identification purposes.

I hereby declare that as the applicant for a certified copy of the above described certificate, I have direct interest in the matter recorded and that the information therein contained is necessary for determination of personal or property rights, as per K.S.A. 65-2422(c).

....

Signature of person making request_____

Relationship_____ Reason for request_____

PLEASE ENCLOSE SELF-ADDRESSED STAMPED ENVELOPE

Number of copies_____

Total fee enclosed $_____

(All fees expire 12 months from date paid.)

PLEASE PRINT CORRECT MAILING ADDRESS:

Date of request_____

_____
(Name)

_____
(Street Address)

_____
(City)   (State)   (Zip)

Form VS-237 Rev 7-1983

KANSAS STATE DEPARTMENT OF HEALTH AND ENVIRONMENT

Vital Statistics

APPLICATION FOR CERTIFIED COPY OF DEATH CERTIFICATE

Death Certificates are on file from July 1, 1911. Provisions of K.A.R. 28-17-6 require a fee of   for the first certified copy of a death certificate and for each additional copy of the same certificate ordered at the same time. Check or money order should be made payable to the State Registrar of Vital Statistics. Cash sent by mail will be at applicant's risk.

_____

FACTS CONCERNING THIS DEATH

Full name of deceased_____

Place of death_____Date of death_____
        (City)   (County)   (State)   (Month) (Day) (Year)

               (ADDITIONAL INFORMATION, IF KNOWN)

Age at time of death_____Place of birth_____
  (or birthdate)

Name of husband or maiden name of wife_____

Usual place of residence_____

Funeral Director's name_____

NOTICE: It is a violation of State and Federal Laws for anyone to make, sell, or offer for sale any death record for false identification purposes.

. . . .

I hereby declare that as the applicant for a certified copy of the above described certificate, I have direct interest in the matter recorded and that the information therein contained is necessary for determination of personal or property rights, as per K.S.A. 65-2422(c).

Signature of person making request_____

                                    Reason
Relationship_____for request_____

```
+---------------------------------------+
|   PLEASE ENCLOSE SELF-ADDRESSED       |      Number of copies_____
|         STAMPED ENVELOPE              |
+---------------------------------------+
```

PLEASE PRINT CORRECT MAILING ADDRESS: Total fee enclosed $_____
                                 (All fees expire 12 months from date paid.)

_____
          (Name)

_____ Date of request_____
      (Street Address)

_____
 (City)   (State)   (Zip Code)

Form VS-236 Rev 7-1983

KENTUCKY

Send your requests to:

Cabinet for Human Services
Department for Health Services
Office of Vital Statistics
275 East Main Street
Frankfort, Kentucky 40621

(606) 564-4212

Cost for a certified Birth Certificate	$5.00
Cost for a wallet size Birth Certificate	$5.00
Cost for a certified Marriage Certificate	$4.00
Cost for a certified Death Certificate	$4.00

The Kentucky Office of Vital Statistics has birth and death records from January 1, 1911. They hold marriage records from June 1, 1958.

COMMONWEALTH OF KENTUCKY
DEPARTMENT FOR HEALTH SERVICES

APPLICATION FOR BIRTH CERTIFICATE

Please Print or Type All Information Required on This Form

Full Name at Birth _____ Sex _____

Date of Birth _____ Ky. County of Birth _____

Mother's Full Maiden Name _____

Father's Name _____

Name of Attending Physician or Midwife _____ Hospital _____

Has Original Certificate Been Changed? If So, To _____

Have You Ever Received a Copy Before? ☐ Yes ☐ No ☐ Unknown

If yes, When? _____
　　　　　　　　　　Year

Please State Purpose For Which This Certificate Is Needed: _____

_____

_____ Phone: _____
(Signature of Applicant)　　　　　(Area Code)　(Number)

Relationship to Person Named on Certificate _____

Office Use Only

Vol. _____

Cert. _____

Year _____

Date _____

Initials _____

Check Type of
Copy desired

☐ Full Size Copy -　　Quantity Desired _____

☐ Billfold Size Birth Card -　　- Quantity Desired _____

Print Name and Mailing Address of Person to Receive the Certificate.
This Portion is a Mailing Insert and Will be Used to Mail the Copy
you Have Requested.

_____
Name

_____
Street Number & Name

_____
City — State — Zip Code

APPLICANT'S PHONE. _____
　　　　　　　　　　　(Area Code)　　(Number)

COMMONWEALTH OF KENTUCKY
DEPARTMENT FOR HEALTH SERVICES

275 EAST MAIN STREET
FRANKFORT, KENTUCKY 40621

VS-230
(Rev. 2-83)

APPLICATION FOR MARRIAGE/DIVORCE CERTIFICATE

Please Print or Type All Information Given on This Form.

It must be clear which information you are requesting—whether marriage or divorce. Please circle the appropriate reference each place required below. Accurate information is necessary to enable us to locate the certificate you are requesting.

Full Name of Husband _____

Maiden Name of Wife _____

County In Which   (Marriage License)   (Divorce Decree)   Granted _____
                              (Circle One)

Date of   (Marriage) (Divorce) _____
                   (Circle One)   (Mo.)   (Day)   (Year)

Name of Applicant _____

Address _____
              (Street No.)   (City)   (State)   (Zip Code)

The Information I Am Requesting Concerns
(Marriage) (Divorce)
(Circle One)

Please Indicate Quantity Desired _____

Office Use Only
Vol. _____
Cert. _____
Year _____
Date _____
Initials _____

Print Name and Mailing Address of Person to Receive the Certificate.
This Portion is a Mailing Insert and Will be Used to Mail the Copy you Have Requested.

_____
Name

_____
Street Number & Name

_____
City—State—Zip Code

VS-31
(Rev. 1-85)

COMMONWEALTH OF KENTUCKY
DEPARTMENT FOR HEALTH SERVICES

APPLICATION FOR DEATH CERTIFICATE

Please Print or Type All Information Required on This Form.

Full Name of Deceased _____

Date of Death _____ KY County in Which
             (Mo.)   (Day)   (Year)   Death Occurred _____

Did Death Occur ☐ ☐ If "Yes" Give
In a Hospital?   Yes No Name of Hospital _____

Name of Attending Physician _____

Name of Funeral Director _____

| Office Use Only |

Address _____
      (Street)   (City)   (State)   Vol. _____

Name of Applicant _____   Cert. _____

Address _____   Year _____
      (Street)   (City)   (State)   Date _____

_____ Phone _____
   Signature of Applicant   (Area Code) (Number)   Initials _____

Please Indicate Quantity Desired _____

Print Name and Mailing Address of Person to Receive the Certificate.
This Portion is a Mailing Insert and Will be Used to Mail the Copy
you Have Requested.

_____
Name

_____
Street Number & Name

_____
City — State — Zip Code

LOUISIANA

Send your requests to:

Louisiana State Department of Health
  and Human Resources
Office of Preventive and Public Health Services
Vital Records Registry
P.O. Box 60630
New Orleans, Louisiana 70160

(504) 568-5152

Cost for a certified Birth Certificate	$8.00
Cost for a wallet size Birth Certificate	$3.00
Cost for a certified Marriage Certificate	$5.00
Cost for a certified Death Certificate	$5.00

The Louisiana Vital Records Registry has state-wide records from July 1, 1914. They also hold New Orleans birth records from 1790 and death records from 1803.

DEPARTMENT OF HEALTH AND HUMAN RESOURCES
OFFICE OF PREVENTIVE AND PUBLIC HEALTH SERVICES
VITAL RECORDS REGISTRY

APPLICATION FOR CERTIFIED COPY OF BIRTH CERTIFICATE

PHS 520A   (Rev. 4/85)

TO REQUEST SERVICE BY MAIL, SUBMIT CHECK OR MONEY ORDER PAYABLE TO VITAL RECORDS.
CASH IS SENT AT YOUR OWN RISK.
IF NO RECORD IS FOUND, YOU WILL BE NOTIFIED AND FEES WILL BE RETAINED FOR THE SEARCH.

☐ BIRTHCARD (For sample see back side of this form.)
☐ BIRTH CERTIFICATE

_____
Name at Birth

_____
Date of Birth (If Unknown Give Approximate Age)

_____
City or Parish of Birth

_____
Father's Name

_____
Mother's Name (Before Marriage)

HOW ARE YOU RELATED TO THE PERSON WHOSE RECORD YOU ARE REQUESTING? _____

WRITE YOUR ADDRESS (FOR OUR RECORDS ONLY)

Name _____   Number of Copies
Street or   of each Certificate
Route No. _____   Requested: _____
City
and State _____   Total Fees Due $ _____
                        Zip Code

I AM AWARE THAT ANY PERSON WHO WILLFULLY AND KNOWINGLY MAKES ANY FALSE STATEMENT IN
AN APPLICATION FOR A CERTIFIED COPY OF A VITAL RECORD IS SUBJECT UPON CONVICTION TO
A FINE OF NOT MORE THAN $10,000 OR IMPRISONMENT OF NOT MORE THAN FIVE YEARS, OR BOTH.

(PLEASE DO NOT WRITE IN THIS SPACE)   _____
                                                   Signature of Applicant
CLIENT WAITING   _____
CLIENT WILL PICK UP   _____
NEXT DAY MAIL OUT   _____   _____
TIME IN   _____   Home Phone Number
TIME OUT   _____
                                                   _____
                                                   Office Phone Number

DEPARTMENT OF HEALTH AND HUMAN RESOURCES
OFFICE OF PREVENTIVE AND PUBLIC HEALTH SERVICES
VITAL RECORDS REGISTRY

APPLICATION FOR CERTIFIED COPY OF MARRIAGE CERTIFICATE

PHS 520C   (Rev. 5/85)

TO REQUEST SERVICE BY MAIL, SUBMIT CHECK OR MONEY ORDER PAYABLE TO VITAL RECORDS.
CASH IS SENT AT YOUR OWN RISK.
IF NO RECORD IS FOUND, YOU WILL BE NOTIFIED AND FEES WILL BE RETAINED FOR THE SEARCH.

MARRIAGE RECORD OF:

_____
Groom

_____
Bride

_____
Parish where License was Purchased

_____
Date of Marriage

PLEASE NOTE: A MARRIAGE RECORD IS AVAILABLE FROM THE DIVISION OF VITAL RECORDS ONLY IF THE MARRIAGE LICENSE WAS PURCHASED IN ORLEANS PARISH. OTHERWISE YOU MUST CONTACT THE CLERK OF COURT IN THE PARISH WHERE THE LICENSE WAS PURCHASED.

WRITE YOUR ADDRESS (FOR OUR RECORDS ONLY)

Name _____   Number of Copies
                                          of each Certificate
Street or   Requested: _____
Route No. _____

City   Total Fees Due $_____
and State _____
                          Zip Code

PLEASE MAIL FORM TO:

LOUISIANA VITAL RECORDS SECTION
P. O. BOX 60630
NEW ORLEANS, LOUISIANA 70160

PLEASE FILL OUT THE ADDRESS BELOW ONLY IF THE CERTIFICATE IS TO BE MAILED

Certificate to be mailed to:

Name _____
Street or
Route No. _____
City
and State _____
                          Zip Code

APPLICATION FOR CERTIFIED COPY OF DEATH CERTIFICATE

PHS 520B   (Rev. 5/85)

TO REQUEST SERVICE BY MAIL, SUBMIT CHECK OR MONEY ORDER PAYABLE TO VITAL RECORDS.
CASH IS SENT AT YOUR OWN RISK.
IF NO RECORD IS FOUND, YOU WILL BE NOTIFIED AND FEES WILL BE RETAINED FOR THE SEARCH.

DEATH RECORD OF:

_____

Name at Death

_____

Date of Death

_____

City or Parish of Death

HOW ARE YOU RELATED TO THE PERSON WHOSE RECORD YOU ARE REQUESTING? _____

WRITE YOUR ADDRESS (FOR OUR RECORDS ONLY)

Name _____   Number of Copies
                                                of each Certificate
Street or   Requested: _____
Route No. _____

City
and State _____   Total Fees Due $ _____
                        Zip Code

- -

PLEASE MAIL FORM TO:

LOUISIANA VITAL RECORDS SECTION
P. O. BOX 60630
NEW ORLEANS, LOUISIANA 70160

PLEASE FILL OUT THE ADDRESS BELOW ONLY IF THE CERTIFICATE IS TO BE MAILED

Certificate to be mailed to: _____

Name _____

Street or
Route No. _____

City
and State _____
                        Zip Code

MAINE

Send your requests to:

Maine Department of Human Services
Office of Vital Statistics
(221 State Street)
State House, Station 11
Augusta, Maine 04333

(207) 289-3184

Cost for a certified Birth Certificate	$5.00
Cost for a certified Marriage Certificate	$5.00
Cost for a certified Death Certificate	$5.00
Cost for a duplicate copy, when ordered at the same time	$2.00

The Maine Office of Vital Statistics has records from January 1, 1892. Make your check payable to "Treasurer, State of Maine."

If your request is urgent you may call and charge your certificates to your visa or mastercard. There is a $6.00 fee for this service.

APPLICATION FOR A SEARCH AND A CERTIFIED COPY OF A RECORD

Make Checks Payable to-"TREASURER OF STATE OF MAINE"

DEPARTMENT OF HUMAN SERVICES
OFFICE OF VITAL STATISTICS
STATE HOUSE STATION 11
AUGUSTA, MAINE 04333

 This application should be sent to this address.

Applicant: Please fill in the information in the appropriate box for the record you are requesting, the reason for requesting the record, and the name and address for mailing the certified copy.

BIRTH RECORD

| Full Name of Child |
| Date of Birth |
| Place of Birth |
| Father's Full Name |
| Mother's Maiden Name |

DEATH RECORD

| Full Name of Decedent |
| Date of Death |
| Place of Death |

MARRIAGE RECORD

| Full Name of Groom |
| Full Maiden Name of Bride |
| Date of Marriage |
| Place of Marriage |

Reason for requesting record: _____

Print or type name and address to whom the record is to be sent.

VS-107
Rev, 1/85

Signature of Applicant:_____

MARYLAND

Send your requests to:

Maryland Department of Health & Mental Hygiene
Division of Vital Records
State Office Building
P.O. Box 13146
Baltimore, Maryland 21203

(301) 225-5971

Cost for a certified Birth Certificate	$3.00
Cost for a wallet size Birth Certificate	$3.00
Cost for a certified Marriage Certificate	$3.00
Cost for a certified Death Certificate	$3.00
Cost for a duplicate copy, when ordered at the same time	$3.00

The Maryland Division of Vital Records has birth and death records from August 1, 1898 and marriage records from June 1, 1951. They also hold birth and death records for Baltimore from January 1, 1875.

If your request is urgent you may call and charge your certificates to your visa or mastercard. There is a $6.00 fee for this service, plus the postal charges.

STATE OF MARYLAND
DEPARTMENT OF HEALTH & MENTAL HYGIENE
Division of Vital Records
P.O. Box 13146
Baltimore, Maryland 21203

Send Check or Postal Money Order Payable to
DEPARTMENT OF HEALTH & MENTAL HYGIENE.

DO NOT WRITE IN ABOVE SPACE.

APPLICATION FOR A COPY OR ABSTRACT OF CERTIFICATE OF BIRTH

Date _____ 19 __

Full name at birth: _____ Sex: _____

Date of birth: _____ Age last birthday: _____
Certificate No.
(If known): _____

Place of birth: _____ County: _____

Name of Hospital (If known): _____

Number of child in order of birth: _____

Full name of father: _____

Full maiden name of mother: _____

Present address of parents: _____

Reason for request: _____

Your relationship to person whose birth record is requested: _____

IMPORTANT: INDICATE BY CHECKMARK BELOW THE TYPE OF RECORD TO BE ISSUED.

/___/ CERTIFIED PHOTOCOPY: This can be used for all purposes.

/___/ WALLET-SIZE BIRTH CARD: This card can be used for all purposes
except legal cases.

SIGNATURE OF APPLICANT_____
MAILING ADDRESS_____
CITY & STATE_____
ZIP CODE_____
ENCLOSE SELF-ADDRESSED STAMPED ENVELOPE

DHMH 1526
VR C-31
05/86 - 15M

STATE OF MARYLAND
DEPARTMENT OF HEALTH & MENTAL HYGIENE
Division of Vital Records
P.O. Box 13146
Baltimore, Maryland 21203

No. Copies _____

Date Issued _____

SEND CHECK OR POSTAL MONEY ORDER PAYABLE TO
DEPARTMENT OF HEALTH & MENTAL HYGIENE

DO NOT WRITE IN THE ABOVE SPACE.

APPLICATION FOR CERTIFIED COPY OF MARRIAGE CERTIFICATE

NOTE: For marriages performed <u>PRIOR TO JUNE, 1951</u>, verifications or certified copies of the certificates are available ONLY from the Circuit Court of the County in which the marriage took place.

DATE _____ 19___

GROOM'S NAME _____
          (First)   (Middle)   (Last)

BRIDE'S MAIDEN NAME _____
          (First)   (Middle)   (Last)

DATE OF MARRIAGE _____
          (Month)   (Day)   (Year)

PLACE OF MARRIAGE _____
          (Town)   (County)

WHO DO YOU REPRESENT _____

FOR WHAT PURPOSE DESIRED _____

APPLICANT'S NAME _____
                              (Print)

APPLICANT'S SIGNATURE _____

FULL MAILING ADDRESS _____
          (Number)   (Street)

_____
   (City)   (State)   (Zip Code)

<u>ENCLOSE SELF-ADDRESSED STAMPED ENVELOPE FOR FAST SERVICE.</u>

VR C80
DHMH 1937
06/86-5M

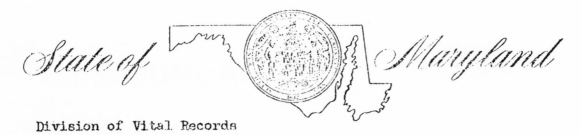

State of Maryland

Division of Vital Records

DEPARTMENT OF HEALTH AND MENTAL HYGIENE

Relative to your application for a certified copy of a Certificate of Death please be advised that it will be necessary for you to fill out the application below, and either mail or bring it to this office.

APPLICATION FOR CERTIFIED COPY OF DEATH CERTIFICATE

PLEASE NOTE CAREFULLY: A fee of   is required, in advance, FOR A SEARCH of the files. If the record is found, one copy will be issued without further charge. Additional copies of the same record issued at the same time may be obtained at the rate of   each. Please make checks or money orders payable to the Department of Health & Mental Hygiene.
DO NOT SEND CASH OR STAMPS.

Date_____ 19____

Name of deceased _____
                         (First)   (Middle)   (Last)

Date of death _____
                         (Month)   (Day)   (Year)

Place of death regardless of residence _____
                                              (Town)   (County)

Number of copies desired _____. For what purpose desired _____.

Your name _____

Your address _____
                         (Number)   (Street)

              _____
                  (City or Town)   (State)   (Zip Code)
ENCLOSE SELF-ADDRESSED STAMPED ENVELOPE FOR FAST SERVICE.

VR C34
10/85 - 5M

MASSACHUSETTS

Send your requests to:

Massachusetts Executive Office of Human Services
Division of Health Statistics and Research
Registry of Vital Records and Statistics
150 Tremont Street, Room B-3
Boston, Massachusetts 02111

(617) 727-0036

Cost for a certified Birth Certificate	$3.00
Cost for a certified Marriage Certificate	$3.00
Cost for a certified Death Certificate	$3.00
Cost for a duplicate copy, when ordered at the same time	$3.00

The Massachusetts Registry of Vital Records and Statistics has records from January 1, 1891. The Registry does not currently provide application forms for vital records but requests that you simply state your request in a brief letter.

MICHIGAN

Send your requests to:

Michigan Department of Public Health
Office of the State Registrar
  and Center for Health Statistics
3428 North Logan Street
P.O. Box 30035
Lansing, Michigan 48909

(517) 335-8656

Cost for a certified Birth Certificate	$10.00
Cost for a certified Marriage Certificate	$10.00
Cost for a certified Death Certificate	$10.00
Cost for a duplicate copy, when ordered at the same time	$ 3.00

The Michigan State Registrar has birth and death records from January 1, 1867 and marriage records from April 1867. If you are doing genealogical research the fee for the first record requested is $10.00, and the additional records requested are $6.00 each if requested in the same envelope.

If your request is urgent you may call and charge your certificates to your visa or mastercard. There is a $5.00 fee for this service, plus the postal charges.

APPLICATION FOR A CERTIFICATE OF REGISTRATION OR A
CERTIFIED COPY OF A BIRTH RECORD

PRINT CLEARLY

1. Name at Birth_____   Date of
   Or adopted name: ____First____Middle____Last____   Birth: _____
                                                                        Mo   Day   Year

2. Place of Birth: _____
               Hospital (if known)   City   County

3. Mother's Maiden Name: _____
                  First   Middle   Last

4. Father's Name: _____
             First   Middle   Last

5. Is the individual named in No. 1 adopted?   ☐ yes   ☐ no   ☐ maybe
   If the information is available and you are the individual named in No. 1, or if the record is being sent to the individual named in No. 1, do you wish to receive the name and location of the court where the adoption took place?   ☐ yes   ☐ no

6.
   > PLEASE PROVIDE IN THIS SPACE ANY ADDITIONAL INFORMATION THAT WOULD HELP US LOCATE THE RECORD, FOR EXAMPLE, A LEGAL CHANGE OF NAME

RECORDS CAN BE PROVIDED ONLY TO ELIGIBLE PERSONS (SEE INSTRUCTIONS ON REVERSE.)

7. Please place an "X" in the appropriate area and follow additional instructions.
   My Relationship To The Person In Line 1 Is:

☐ INDIVIDUAL NAMED IN LINE 1	☐ PARENT NAMED ON RECORD ☐ LEGAL GUARDIAN

   ☐ LEGAL REPRESENTATIVE — Whom Are You Representing? _____
   ☐ HEIR — Specify Your Relationship To The Person In Line 1? _____

   > IF YOU STATE YOUR RELATIONSHIP AS AN HEIR PLEASE PROVIDE THE DATE AND PLACE OF DEATH OF THE PERSON NAMED IN LINE 1
   >
   > _____
   > DATE
   >
   > _____
   > PLACE

8. Applicant's
   Signature:_____
            Signature of Applicant   Date

   Applicant's
   Address:_____
          Street   City   State   Zip   Area Code   Phone

   (APPLICATION MUST BE SIGNED TO PROCESS YOUR REQUEST)

THIS BOX FOR INTERNAL USE ONLY	DP INFORMATION
	YEAR ....
	REGISTRATION NUMBER
	_____

(PLEASE DO NOT REMOVE THIS STUB)

PRINT THE NAME AND MAILING ADDRESS OF THE PERSON
TO WHOM THE RECORD(S) ARE TO BE SENT.

**THIS IS A MAILING INSERT AND WILL BE USED
TO MAIL THE RECORDS**

9. Name: _____
   Street: _____
   City: _____
   State: _____   Zip: _____

APPLICATION FOR A CERTIFIED COPY OF A MARRIAGE CERTIFICATE

We are required by Act 368 of 1978 as amended, to collect the statutory fee before a search may be made for any record. Fee schedule is itemized below. Please make check or money order payable to the STATE OF MICHIGAN.

Minimum fee for ONE CERTIFIED COPY — Minimum fee includes a 3 year search	
ADDITIONAL CERTIFIED COPIES of the same record ordered at the same time —	
ADDITIONAL YEARS searched over 3 years — each (when exact year is not known and more than a 3 year search is required, remit — FOR EACH additional year over the minimum 3 years searched)	
TOTAL	

FEES PAID TO SEARCH THE FILES ARE NOT REFUNDABLE.

When a record is not found, the applicant will receive notification that the record as requested is not on file in this office.

PLEASE PRINT

Please send me a certified copy of the marriage certificate of:

Name of groom _____

Name of bride at time of
application for marriage license _____

Date of marriage _____
(Month)   (Day)   (Year)

If exact year is unknown _____
(Years to be searched)

Place where license was obtained _____
(County)

_____   _____
Applicant's Signature   Date

(PLEASE DO NOT REMOVE THIS STUB)

PRINT THE NAME AND MAILING ADDRESS OF THE PERSON TO WHOM THE RECORD(S) ARE TO BE SENT.

THIS IS A MAILING INSERT AND WILL BE USED TO MAIL THE RECORDS.

ADDITIONAL INFORMATION

NAME _____

STREET _____

CITY _____

STATE _____ ZIP _____

B-225-C 10/84

MICHIGAN DEPARTMENT OF PUBLIC HEALTH
Office of the State Registrar and Center for Health Statistics

P.O. Box 30035
Lansing, MI 48909

APPLICATION FOR A CERTIFIED COPY OF A DEATH CERTIFICATE

We are required by Act 368 of 1978 as amended, to collect the statutory fee before a search may be made for any record. Fee schedule is itemized below. Please make check or money order payable to the STATE OF MICHIGAN.

Minimum fee for ONE CERTIFIED COPY — Minimum fee includes a 3 year search	
ADDITIONAL CERTIFIED COPIES of the same record ordered at the same time —	
ADDITIONAL YEARS searched over 3 years — (when exact year is not known and more than a 3 year search is required, remit — FOR EACH additional year over the minimum 3 years searched	
TOTAL	

FEES PAID TO SEARCH THE FILES ARE NOT REFUNDABLE

WHEN A RECORD IS NOT FOUND, THE APPLICANT WILL RECEIVE NOTIFICATION THAT THE RECORD AS REQUESTED IS NOT ON FILE IN THIS OFFICE.

PLEASE PRINT

Please send me a certified copy of the death certificate of:

Name of deceased: _____
(First)   (Middle)   (Last)

Date of death: _____
(Month)   (Day)   (Year)

If exact year is unknown: _____
(Years to be searched)

Place of death _____
(Township, Village, or City)   (County)

_____
Applicant's Signature   Date

IF THE INFORMATION REQUESTED ABOVE IS NOT KNOWN, please indicate in the box below any which may be used for identifying the record, such as marital status, name of husband or wife if married, parents' name birthplace.

- - - - (PLEASE DO NOT REMOVE THIS STUB) - - - -

PRINT THE NAME AND MAILING ADDRESS OF THE PERSON TO WHOM THE RECORD(S) ARE TO BE SENT.
THIS IS A MAILING INSERT AND WILL BE USED TO MAIL THE RECORDS

ADDITIONAL INFORMATION

NAME: _____

STREET: _____

CITY: _____

STATE: _____ ZIP: _____

B-225B 12/84

APPLICATION TO REQUEST A VITAL RECORD FOR GENEALOGICAL RESEARCH

By Law, the statutory fee must be paid before a search may be made for any Record. The fee schedule is itemized below. Please make check or money order payable to STATE OF MICHIGAN. FEES ARE NOT REFUNDABLE.

	NUMBER	FEE
1. First record request — fee includes 3 year search		
Second and subsequent record requests submitted at the same time in the same envelope		
Additional copies of the same record ordered at the same time		
Additional years searched per record request		
GENEALOGICAL RESEARCH COPIES ARE NON-CERTIFIED	TOTAL	

2. **RECORD TYPE:** ☐ Death   ☐ Marriage   ☐ Divorce

☐ Birth { You must satisfy the eligibility requirements required by law and supply the following information: (See other side for instructions)

3) Your relationship to person named on the birth record _____

4) The date and place the person named on the birth record died _____

date

_____

place

5. _____
name of registrant; name of deceased; name of groom; name of husband
(birth)   (death)   (marriage)   (divorce)

6. Date of Event: _____   7. Place of Event: _____
(city, village, township and county)

8. If exact year is unknown, years to be searched: _____

9. _____
mother's maiden name; name of bride; name of wife
(birth)   (marriage)   (divorce)

10. Father's name (birth only): _____

11. Applicant's Signature: _____   Date: _____

IF THE INFORMATION REQUESTED ABOVE IS NOT KNOWN, please indicate in the box below any data which may be used for identifying the record, such as marital status, name of husband or wife if married, parents' names, age or birthplace.

- -

(PLEASE DO NOT REMOVE THIS STUB)

PRINT THE NAME AND MAILING ADDRESS OF THE PERSON TO WHOM THE RECORD(S) ARE TO BE SENT.
THIS IS A MAILING INSERT AND WILL BE USED TO MAIL THE RECORDS

NAME: _____

STREET: _____

CITY: _____   STATE: _____   ZIP: _____

ADDITIONAL INFORMATION

B 225 G 3/85

Authority: ACT 368, P.A. 1978
Completion: Voluntary

MINNESOTA

Send your requests to:

Minnesota Department of Health
Section of Vital Statistics Registration
717 Delaware Street, S.E.
P.O. Box 9441
Minneapolis, Minnesota 55440

(612) 623-5121

Send your requests for Marriage Certificates to:

Clerk
County District Court
(County where the Marriage License was issued)

Cost for a certified Birth Certificate	$11.00
Cost for a duplicate Birth Certificate	$ 5.00
Cost for a certified Death Certificate	$ 8.00
Cost for a duplicate death certificate, when ordered at the same time	$ 2.00

The Minnesota Section of Vital Statistics Registration has birth records from January 1, 1900 and death records from January 1, 1908.

If your request is urgent you may call and charge your certificates to your visa or mastercard. There is a $5.00 fee for this service.

1. Our files include birth records since 1900 and death records since 1908 for the entire State of Minnesota. Some records prior to these years are on file with the clerk of District Court in the county of occurrence.

2. Minnesota law requires a fee of   for each certified copy of a record, non-certified copy of a record, verification, or statement that the record is not on file.

3. A check or money order should be made payable to "Treasurer, State of Minnesota". PLEASE NOTE: We cannot accept two-party checks, Canadian checks or Canadian currency.

(A) BIRTH

Name: _____

Date of Birth: _____

City, Town or Township of Birth: _____

County of Birth: _____

Father's Full Name: _____

Mother's Full Maiden Name: _____

(B) DEATH

Name: _____

Date of Death: _____
 (or year last known to be alive)

City, Town or Township of Death: _____

County of Death: _____

Age at the time of Death: _____

Occupation: _____

Spouse's Full Name: _____

(C) ISSUE TO

Signature: _____

Street or Route: _____

City, State & Zip Code: _____

F 117

MISSISSIPPI

Send your requests to:

Mississippi State Department of Health
Vital Records Office
2423 North State Street
P.O. Box 1700
Jackson, Mississippi 39215-1700

(601) 960-7981

Cost for a certified Birth Certificate	$10.00
Cost for a short form Birth Certificate	$ 5.00
Cost for a certified Marriage Certificate	$ 5.00
Cost for a certified Death Certificate	$ 5.00
Cost for a duplicate copy, when ordered at the same time	$ 1.00

The Mississippi Office of Vital Records has birth records from November 1, 1912; marriage records from January 1, 1916 to June 30, 1938 and from January 1, 1942 to the present; and death records from November 1, 1912. The Office will only accept payment by postal money order, bank money order, or by a bank cashier's check.

If your request is urgent you may call and charge your order for birth certificates to your visa or mastercard. There is a $4.50 fee for this service.

MISSISSIPPI STATE DEPARTMENT OF HEALTH

APPLICATION FOR CERTIFIED COPY OF BIRTH CERTIFICATE

INFORMATION	INSTRUCTIONS
Only births recorded after November 1, 1912 are on file.	1. Complete ALL the information sections of the form. PLEASE PRINT. 2. The application must be signed. 3. Please remit a POSTAL MONEY ORDER, BANK MONEY ORDER or BANK CASHIER'S CHECK made payable to the Mississippi State Department of Health. Personal checks and personal money orders are not accepted. <u>We accept no responsibility for cash sent through the mail.</u> 4. Send completed application, appropriate fee and self-addressed stamped legal size envelope to the address at the top of this form.

BASIC INFORMATION: DOUBLE CHECK SPELLING AND DATE				DO NOT WRITE IN THIS SPACE
1. FULL NAME AT BIRTH	FIRST NAME	MIDDLE NAME	LAST NAME	STATE FILE NUMBER
2. DATE OF BIRTH	MONTH	DAY	YEAR	
3. PLACE OF BIRTH	COUNTY	CITY OR TOWN	STATE	FILING DATE

ADDITIONAL INFORMATION REQUIRED:				
4. SEX		5. RACE		12 – 36
				37 – 66
6. FULL NAME OF FATHER	FIRST NAME	MIDDLE NAME	LAST NAME	S.C.
7. FULL MAIDEN NAME OF MOTHER	FIRST NAME	MIDDLE NAME	LAST NAME	S.C.
8. HAS NAME EVER BEEN CHANGED OTHER THAN BY MARRIAGE? Yes ☐ No ☐		IF SO, WHAT WAS ORIGINAL NAME?		S.C.

ABOUT THE APPLICANT:	
	S.C.
9. FEE I AM ENCLOSING FEE OF $ _____ FOR _____ SHORT FORMS.	S.C.
I AM ENCLOSING FEE OF $ _____ FOR _____ LONG FORMS.	C.D.
10. RELATIONSHIP OF APPLICANT TO PERSON NAMED IN ITEM 1.	SUP.
11. PURPOSE FOR WHICH THIS COPY IS REQUESTED	P.
Pursuant to Section 41-57-2 of the Mississippi Code of 1972, as Amended, and as defined by Mississippi State Board of Health Rules and Regulations, I hereby certify that I have a legitimate and tangible interest in the birth record requested. I understand that obtaining a record under false pretenses may subject me to the penalty as described in Section 41-57-27 of the Mississippi Code of 1972, as Amended.	CWA.

12. SIGNATURE OF APPLICANT	DATE SIGNED

PRINT YOUR MAILING ADDRESS HERE

13.		NAME
14.	Apt. No.	Street Or Route
15.		City Or Town State, ZIP Code

MISSISSIPPI STATE BOARD OF HEALTH

APPLICATION FOR CERTIFIED COPY OF STATISTICAL RECORD OF MARRIAGE

INFORMATION

Marriage records have only been kept since January 1, 1926. In addition, from July 1, 1938, to December 31, 1941, records were kept only by the circuit court clerk in the county in which the marriage license was issued.

INSTRUCTIONS

1. Complete the information sections of this form. PLEASE PRINT.
2. The application must be signed.
3. Payment for certificates is preferably by Money Order. Personal checks or cash are not recommended.
4. Send (a) completed application form and
   (b) appropriate fee
to the address at the top of this form.

INFORMATION ABOUT BRIDE AND GROOM WHOSE STATISTICAL RECORD OF MARRIAGE IS REQUESTED (Please Print)			
1. FULL NAME OF GROOM	FIRST NAME	MIDDLE NAME	LAST NAME
2. FULL NAME OF BRIDE	FIRST NAME	MIDDLE NAME	LAST NAME
3. DATE OF MARRIAGE	MONTH	DAY	YEAR
4. PLACE OF MARRIAGE	COUNTY	CITY OR TOWN	STATE
5. WHERE LICENSE WAS BOUGHT	COUNTY	CITY OR TOWN	STATE
PERSON REQUESTING CERTIFIED COPY			
6. PURPOSE FOR WHICH COPY IS TO BE USED			
7. RELATIONSHIP OR INTEREST OF PERSON REQUESTING CERTIFICATE			
8. FEE I AM ENCLOSING A FEE OF $ _____ FOR _____ CERTIFIED COPIES.			
9. SIGNATURE OF APPLICANT		10. DATE SIGNED	

PRINT OR TYPE YOUR MAILING ADDRESS HERE

11.	NAME
12.	Street Or Route
13.	City Or Town / State, ZIP Code

Form No. 523
Revised 3/1/81

MISSISSIPPI STATE BOARD OF HEALTH

APPLICATION FOR CERTIFIED COPY OF DEATH CERTIFICATE
INFORMATION

1. Only deaths recorded after November 1, 1912, are on file.
2. The death certificate is the most important legal document in the settlement of the estate and insurance. It is important that the information on the certificate is correct.
3. When you receive copies of the death certificate, check particularly spelling of names and that dates are correct.
4. If there are any incorrect items on the certificate and the death has occurred less than one year ago, please notify the funeral director who filed the certificate.
5. If there are incorrect items on the certificate and the death occurred more than one year ago, a court order is required. Please contact Vital Records at the above address for additional information.

INSTRUCTIONS

1. Complete the information sections of this form. PLEASE PRINT.
2. The application must be signed.
3. Payment for certificates is preferably by Money Order. Personal checks or cash are not recommended.
4. Send (a) completed application form and
       (b) appropriate fee
   to the address at the top of this form.

INFORMATION ABOUT PERSON WHOSE DEATH CERTIFICATE IS REQUESTED (Type or Print)		
1. FULL NAME OF DECEASED — FIRST NAME	MIDDLE NAME	LAST NAME
2. DATE OF DEATH — MONTH	DAY	YEAR
3. PLACE OF DEATH — COUNTY	CITY OR TOWN	STATE
4. SEX 5. RACE	6. AGE AT DEATH	7. STATE FILE NUMBER IF KNOWN
8. NAME OF FATHER	9. NAME OF MOTHER	
10. FUNERAL DIRECTOR — NAME	ADDRESS	
11. PURPOSE FOR WHICH CERTIFIED COPY IS TO BE USED	NO. OF COPIES	
12. RELATIONSHIP OR INTEREST OF PERSON REQUESTING CERTIFICATE	VETERAN'S SERVICE OR VA CLAIM NO.	
13. SIGNATURE OF APPLICANT	TOTAL	
14. DATE SIGNED	FEE SUBMITTED .... $	

PRINT OR TYPE YOUR MAILING ADDRESS HERE

15.		NAME
16.		Street Or Route
17.		City Or Town State, ZIP Code

MISSOURI

Send your requests to:

Missouri Department of Health
Bureau of Vital Records
P.O. Box 570
Jefferson City, Missouri 65102

(314) 751-6387

Send your requests for Marriage Certificates to:

Recorder of Deeds
County Court House
(County where the Marriage License was issued)

Cost for a certified Birth Certificate	$4.00
Cost for a wallet size Birth Certificate	$4.00
Cost for a certified Death Certificate	$4.00

The Missouri Bureau of Vital Records has birth and death records from January 1, 1910. They also have an index to marriages from July 1, 1948; however, marriage certificates can only be obtained from the county courts. The Bureau will search this index for free.

If your request is urgent you may call and charge your birth certificates to your visa or mastercard. There is a $5.00 fee for this service.

MISSOURI DEPARTMENT OF HEALTH
BUREAU OF VITAL RECORDS
Jefferson City, Missouri 65102

APPLICATION FOR CERTIFIED COPY OF BIRTH CERTIFICATION

INSTRUCTIONS	COPIES REQUESTED

INSTRUCTIONS

NO CASH BY MAIL PLEASE. Make check or money order payable to *Missouri Department of Health.*

Mail this application to:

Missouri Department of Health
Bureau of Vital Records
P. O. Box 570
Jefferson City, Missouri 65102-0570

COPIES REQUESTED

Birth Certification   How Many
Certification of facts of birth contained in original record.

Birth Card   How Many
A nonlaminated wallet-size card that includes only information shown in sample.

Amount of Money Enclosed $

MISSOURI DEPARTMENT OF HEALTH
BIRTH CERTIFICATION
DATE FILED   STATE FILE NUMBER
June 22, 1955   124-41-42355
CHILD NAME
John Henry Dow
BIRTH DATE   SEX
Feb. 31, 1984   M
COUNTY OF BIRTH
Butler
DATE ISSUED
March 9, 1999

THIS IS A TRUE CERTIFICATION OF NAME AND BIRTH FACTS RECORDED IN THIS STATE
THE REPRODUCTION OF THIS DOCUMENT IS PROHIBITED BY LAW. ANY ALTERATION OR ERASURE VOIDS THIS CERTIFICATION

INFORMATION ABOUT PERSON WHOSE BIRTH CERTIFICATE IS REQUESTED *(TYPE or PRINT all items EXCEPT SIGNATURE)*

1. FULL NAME OF PERSON	FIRST NAME	MIDDLE NAME	LAST NAME	
2. DATE OF BIRTH	MONTH	DAY	YEAR	3. SEX	4. RACE
5. PLACE OF BIRTH	CITY OR TOWN	COUNTY	STATE	
	HOSPITAL OR STREET NO.	ATTENDING PHYSICIAN	PHYSICIAN ☐ MIDWIFE ☐ OTHER ☐	
6. FULL NAME OF FATHER	FIRST NAME	MIDDLE NAME	LAST NAME	
7. FULL MAIDEN NAME OF MOTHER	FIRST NAME	MIDDLE NAME	LAST NAME (MAIDEN)	

PERSON REQUESTING CERTIFIED COPY

8. PURPOSE FOR WHICH CERTIFIED COPY IS TO BE USED	
9. RELATIONSHIP *(must be registrant, member of immediate family, legal guardian, or legal representative)*	
10. SIGNATURE OF APPLICANT	11. DATE SIGNED
12. ADDRESS OF APPLICANT *(TYPE or PRINT)*	STREET ADDRESS
	CITY OR TOWN	STATE	ZIP CODE

THIS COUPON MUST BE COMPLETED AND WILL BE USED TO ADDRESS OUR REPLY.

Your fee receipt is on reverse side.

Please print or type the name and address of the person to whom the record is to be furnished.

Name of Person certification is requested for:

_____
NAME

_____   _____
NUMBER   STREET

_____   _____   _____
CITY   STATE   ZIP CODE

MO 580-0641 (10-85)

VS-151 (R10-85)

APPLICATION FOR CERTIFIED COPY OF DEATH CERTIFICATION

INSTRUCTIONS

No Cash Please. Make check or money order payable to:
Missouri Department of Health

Mail this application to:
Missouri Department of Health
Bureau of Vital Records
P. O. Box 570
Jefferson City, Missouri 65102-0570

COPIES REQUESTED

Death Certification   How Many
(Certification of facts of death contained in original record)

Amount of Money Enclosed

THE RECORDING OF DEATHS BEGAN IN THIS OFFICE ON JAN. 1, 1910. RECORDS ARE FILED BY YEAR OF DEATH AND ALPHABETICALLY BY THE NAME OF THE DECEASED AT THE TIME OF DEATH. THEREFORE, AT LEAST THE APPROXIMATE YEAR OF DEATH OR LAST YEAR IN WHICH THE DECEASED WAS KNOWN TO BE ALIVE MUST BE GIVEN.

INFORMATION ABOUT PERSON WHOSE DEATH CERTIFICATE IS REQUESTED *(TYPE or PRINT all items EXCEPT SIGNATURE)*

	FIRST NAME	MIDDLE NAME	LAST NAME AT TIME OF DEATH		
1. FULL NAME OF DECEASED					
2. DATE OF DEATH	MONTH	DAY / YEAR	3. SEX	RACE	AGE
4. PLACE OF DEATH	CITY OR TOWN	COUNTY	STATE		
5. FULL NAME OF SPOUSE	FIRST NAME	MIDDLE NAME	LAST NAME		
6. FULL NAME OF FATHER	FIRST NAME	MIDDLE NAME	LAST NAME		
7. FULL MAIDEN NAME OF MOTHER	FIRST NAME	MIDDLE NAME	LAST NAME (MAIDEN)		

PERSON REQUESTING CERTIFIED COPY OF DEATH RECORD

8. PURPOSE FOR WHICH CERTIFIED COPY IS TO BE USED	Please check: ☐ Insurance claim on policy issued within 2 years of death ☐ Other insurance claims ☐ Other (specify) _____

9. RELATIONSHIP TO REGISTRANT OR INTEREST OF PERSON REQUESTING CERTIFICATION

10. SIGNATURE OF APPLICANT

11. NAME AND ADDRESS WHERE COPIES ARE TO BE MAILED (TYPE or PRINT)	NAME	12. NAME AND ADDRESS OF FUNERAL HOME	
	STREET ADDRESS		13. DATE SIGNED
	CITY OR TOWN	STATE	ZIP CODE

THIS COUPON MUST BE COMPLETED AND WILL BE USED TO ADDRESS OUR REPLY.

Your fee receipt is on reverse side.

Please print or type the name and address of the person to whom the record is to be furnished.

_____
NAME

Name of person certificate is requested for:

_____

NUMBER   STREET

CITY   STATE   ZIP CODE

MO 580-0640 (9-85)

VS-351 (R9-85)

MONTANA

Send your requests to:

Montana Department of Health
and Environmental Sciences
Bureau of Records and Statistics
Cogswell Building
Helena, Montana 59620

(406) 444-2614

Send your requests for Marriage Certificates to:

Clerk
County District Court
(County where the Marriage License was issued)

Cost for a certified Birth Certificate $5.00

Cost for a certified Death Certificate $5.00

The Montana Bureau of Records has birth and death records from late 1907.

If your request is urgent you may call and charge your certificates to your visa or mastercard. There is a $5.00 charge for this service.

DEPARTMENT OF HEALTH AND ENVIRONMENTAL SCIENCES

COGSWELL BUILDING

STATE OF MONTANA

HELENA, MONTANA 59620

In reply to your letter, please be advised that the Montana Department of Health and Environmental Sciences requires a fee of _____ in U.S. funds for each certified copy of a birth or death record. If the year of birth or death is not known, there is a fee of _____ per hour or fraction thereof to search our records. Please state the years you wish us to search. If you have urgent need for the certified copy(ies) and you have MasterCard or a Visa card, we can provide same-day service. Call us at (406) 444-2614. The fee for the certified copy(ies), special mailing costs (if desired), and a _____ service charge will be included on your MasterCard or Visa statement.

PLEASE RETURN THIS LETTER WHEN SENDING THE FEE.

Sincerely,

Charles F. Stohl

Charles F. Stohl
Chief, Fiscal Services Bureau

If the request pertains to a birth, please fill out the top portion. If it pertains to a death, please fill out both portions.

FULL NAME _____

DATE OF BIRTH _____ PLACE OF BIRTH _____
              Month   Day   Year

FATHER'S NAME _____

MOTHER'S MAIDEN NAME _____

DATE OF DEATH _____ PLACE OF DEATH _____
              Month   Day   Year

MARITAL STATUS _____ SPOUSE'S NAME _____

OCCUPATION _____

NEBRASKA

Send your requests to:

Bureau of Vital Statistics
Nebraska State Department of Health
P.O. Box 95007
Lincoln, Nebraska 68509-5007

(402) 471-2871

Cost for a certified Birth Certificate	$6.00
Cost for a wallet size Birth Certificate	$6.00
Cost for a certified Marriage Certificate	$5.00
Cost for a certified Death Certificate	$5.00

The Nebraska Bureau of Vital Statistics has birth and death records from 1904 and marriage records from January 1, 1909.

BVS-C-1
Rev. July 1983
020-08-038

Bureau of Vital Statistics
P. O. Box 95007
Lincoln, Nebraska 68509-5007
(402) 471-2871

APPLICATION FOR BIRTH CERTIFICATE

Nebraska has been registering births with this office since <u>1904</u>. 1941 legislation provided for the filing of delayed birth registrations for births not previously filed; however, there are very few filed for births occurring prior to 1875.

Full name at birth _____
(If adopted, list adoptive name and adoptive parents)

Full date of birth _____

City or county of birth _____

Father's full name _____

Mother's full maiden name _____
Is this the record of an adopted child? _____
Has a delayed birth registration been filed? _____
Purpose record is to be used? _____
How are you related to this person? _____

Certified photocopies   Number _____
Plastic billfold-size birth registration
cards (acceptable for passport purpose)   Number _____

PLEASE ENCLOSE A STAMPED   Signature _____
ADDRESSED ENVELOPE.
                                  Type or print name _____

                                  Firm name _____

                                  Street address _____

Date _____   City, State, Zip _____

Section 71-649, Nebraska Revised Statutes: It is a felony to obtain, possess, use, sell, furnish, or attempt to obtain any vital record for purposes of deception.

BVS-C-6
REV 11/83
020-08-043

Bureau of Vital Statistics
P.O. Box 95007
Lincoln, Nebraska 68509-95007
(402) 471-2871

APPLICATION FOR MARRIAGE RECORD

Nebraska has been registering marriages in this office since 1909. For records occurring prior to that date, contact the county court of the county in which the marriage license was issued.

Full name of groom _____

Full name of bride _____

City of County of marriage _____

Month, day, year of marriage _____

City or county where marriage license issued _____

Purpose record is to be used? _____
If this is not your marriage record, how are you
related to these persons? _____

Signature _____
Typed or printed
name _____

| PLEASE ENCLOSE A STAMPED |
| ADDRESSED ENVELOPE. |

Street address _____

City, State, Zip _____

Section 71-649, Nebraska Revised Statutes: It is a felony to attempt to obtain, possess, or use any copy of a vital record for purposes of deception.

BVS-C-4
Rev. July 1983
020-08-034

BUREAU OF VITAL STATISTICS
P.O. Box 95007
Lincoln, Nebraska 68509-5007
(402)471-2871

APPLICATION FOR DEATH CERTIFICATE

Nebraska has been registering deaths in this office since 1904.

Full name of deceased_____

City or county of death_____

Month, day, year of death_____

Year of birth_____Color_____Birthplace_____

Spouse_____Home address_____

Funeral director:_____

          City_____

For what purpose is record to be used?_____

        Number of certified copies_____

Signature_____

| PLEASE ENCLOSE A STAMPED |
| ADDRESSED ENVELOPE |

Typed or printed
name_____

If to be mailed to another   Firm name_____

address, enter that mailing   Street address_____

address.   City, state, zip_____

Date_____

Name_____
Street address_____
City, state, zip_____

Section 71-649, Nebraska Revised statutes: It is a felony to attempt
to obtain, possess or use any copy of a vital record for purposes of
deception.

Send your requests to:

Nevada State Department of Human Resources
State Health Division
Section of Vital Statistics
505 East King Street
Carson City, Nevada 89710

(702) 885-4480

Send your requests for Marriage Certificates to:

County Recorder
County Court House
(County where the Marriage License was issued)

Cost for a certified Birth Certificate	$6.00
Cost for a wallet size Birth Certificate	$6.00
Cost for a certified Marriage Certificate	$3.00
Cost for a certified Death Certificate	$6.00

The Nevada Section of Vital Statistics has birth and death records from July 1, 1911.

If your request is urgent you may call and charge your certificates to your visa or mastercard. There is a $5.00 fee for this service, plus the postal charges.

NEVADA STATE HEALTH DIVISION
Section of Vital Statistics
Carson City, Nevada 89710
(702) 885-4480

BIRTH CERTIFICATE APPLICATION   No. of Copies____

Search fee when no record is found ...   /name

FULL NAME AT BIRTH_____

DATE of Birth_____

PLACE of Birth_____

Name of Father_____

Maiden Name of Mother_____

Attending Physician or Midwife_____

Purpose for which certificate is to be used_____

_____

_____

Mailing Address_____

_____

Signature of Applicant_____

Relationship_____

XXXXXXXXXXXXXXXXXXXXXXXXXXXXXXXXXXXXXXXXXXXXXXXXXXX

For Office Use Only:

Amount Received_____
Copies Ordered_____
Receipt Number_____   (Date)
Refunded_____

NEVADA STATE HEALTH DIVISION
Section of Vital Statistics
Carson City, Nevada 89710
(702) 885-4480

DEATH CERTIFICATE APPLICATION   No. of Copies___

Search Fee when no record is found -   /name

FULL NAME OF DECEASED_____

Place of Death_____

Date of Death_____

Name of Father of Deceased_____

Maiden Name of Mother_____

Mortuary in Charge of Arrangements_____

Address:_____

Purpose for which certificate is to be used____

_____

Certificate is to be mailed to:_____

_____

Signature of Applicant_____

RELATIONSHIP to Deceased_____

///

For Office use only:

Amount Received:_____   (Date)
Copies Ordered_____
Receipt Number_____
Refunded_____

NEW HAMPSHIRE

Send your requests to:

New Hampshire Division of Public Health
Department of Health and Human Services
Bureau of Vital Records & Health Statistics
6 Hazen Drive
Concord, New Hampshire 03301-6527

(603) 271-4650

Cost for a certified Birth Certificate	$3.00
Cost for a certified Marriage Certificate	$3.00
Cost for a certified Death Certificate	$3.00

New Hampshire has copies of vital records from 1640. Make your check payable to "Treasurer, State of New Hampshire."

If your request is urgent you may call and charge your certificates to your visa or mastercard. There is a $5.00 fee for this service.

BIRTHS

BUREAU OF VITAL RECORDS & HEALTH STATISTICS

CONCORD, NEW HAMPSHIRE 03301
APPLICATION FOR COPY OF BIRTH RETURN

PLEASE PRINT PLAINLY

NAME AT
BIRTH . . . .
                    (FIRST NAME)   (MIDDLE NAME)   (LAST NAME)

DATE OF
BIRTH . . . .
                    (MONTH)   (DAY)   (YEAR)

PLACE OF
BIRTH . . . .

FATHER'S
NAME . . . .
                    (FIRST NAME)   (LAST NAME)

MOTHER'S
MAIDEN NAME . . . .
                    (FIRST NAME)   (LAST NAME)

PURPOSE FOR WHICH CERTIFICATE IS REQUESTED . . . .

BY WHOM . . . . RELATIONSHIP TO REGISTRANT. . . . .

      A FEE OF   **DOLLARS IS REQUIRED BY LAW FOR THE SEARCH OF THE FILE FOR ANY ONE RECORD**

NOTICE: ANY PERSON SHALL BE GUILTY OF A CLASS B FELONY IF HE/SHE WILLFULLY AND KNOWINGLY MAKE ANY FALSE STATEMENT IN AN APPLICATION FOR A CERTIFIED COPY OF A VITAL RECORD. (RSA 126:24)

VS A-1

MARRIAGES

BUREAU OF VITAL RECORDS & HEALTH STATISTICS

NUMBER	
REQUESTED	
ISSUED	

CONCORD, NEW HAMPSHIRE 03301

APPLICATION FOR COPY OF MARRIAGE RETURN

PLEASE PRINT PLAINLY

GROOM'S
NAME . . . .
                      (FIRST NAME)   (LAST NAME)

BRIDE'S
NAME . . . .
                      (FIRST NAME)   (LAST NAME)

DATE OF
MARRIAGE . . . .
                      (MONTH)   (DAY)   (YEAR)

PLACE OF
MARRIAGE . . . .
                                         (COUNTY)

PURPOSE FOR WHICH CERTIFICATE IS REQUESTED . . . .

BY WHOM . . . . RELATIONSHIP TO REGISTRANT . . . .

      A FEE OF   DOLLARS IS REQUIRED BY LAW FOR THE SEARCH OF THE FILE FOR ANY ONE RECORD

NOTICE: ANY PERSON SHALL BE GUILTY OF A CLASS B FELONY IF HE/SHE WILLFULLY AND KNOWINGLY MAKE ANY FALSE STATEMENT IN AN APPLICATION FOR A CERTIFIED COPY OF A VITAL RECORD. (RSA 126:24)

VS B-1

DEATHS

BUREAU OF VITAL RECORDS & HEALTH STATISTICS

CONCORD, NEW HAMPSHIRE 03301

APPLICATION FOR COPY OF DEATH RETURN

PLEASE PRINT PLAINLY

NAME OF
DEASED. . . . .
       (FIRST NAME)   (MIDDLE NAME)   (LAST NAME)

DATE OF
DEATH . . . .
       (MONTH)   (DAY)   (YEAR)

PLACE OF
DEATH . . . .
                (COUNTY)

PURPOSE FOR WHICH CERTIFICATE IS REQUESTED . . . .

BY WHOM . . . . RELATIONSHIP TO REGISTRANT. . . . .

A FEE OF _____ **DOLLARS IS REQUIRED BY LAW FOR THE SEARCH OF THE FILE FOR ANY ONE RECORD**

NOTICE: ANY PERSON SHALL BE GUILTY OF A CLASS B FELONY IF HE/SHE WILLFULLY AND KNOWINGLY MAKE ANY FALSE STATEMENT IN AN APPLICATION FOR A CERTIFIED COPY OF A VITAL RECORD. (RSA 126:24)

VS C-1

NEW JERSEY

Send your requests to:

New Jersey State Department of Health
State Registrar-Search Unit
Bureau of Vital Records
CN 360
Trenton, New Jersey 08625

(609) 292-4087

Send your requests for records from May 1848 to May 1878 to:

Division of Archives and Records Management
Department of State
CN 307
Trenton, New Jersey 08625

(609) 209-6260

Cost for a certified Birth Certificate	$4.00
Cost for a certified Marriage Certificate	$4.00
Cost for a certified Death Certificate	$4.00

Note that there are no state vital records prior to May 1, 1848.

REG-3
Jan. 85

New Jersey State Department of Health

APPLICATION FOR CERTIFIED COPY OF VITAL RECORD

1. VITAL RECORDS - JUNE, 1878 TO PRESENT
   When the correct year of the event is supplied, the total fee (payable in advance) for a search is _____ for each name for which a search must be made. Searches for more than one year cost one dollar for each additional year per name. If found, a certified copy will be forwarded at no additional cost. If not found, the fee will not be refunded. Additional copies may be ordered at this time at a charge of _____ per copy. Specify the total number of copies requested.

2. VITAL RECORDS - MAY, 1848 THROUGH MAY, 1878
   These records have been transferred to the Archives Section, Division of Archives and Records Management, Department of State, CN 307, Trenton, N.J. 08625. Information as to fee schedules and how to obtain records from the Archives can be obtained from that Section.

			FOR STATE USE ONLY
Name of Applicant	Date of Application		
Street Address	Telephone No.		
City	State	Zip Code	Certified Copy Completed

MAKE CHECK OR MONEY ORDER PAYABLE TO "STATE REGISTRAR."
DO NOT MAIL CASH OR STAMPS. PLEASE PRINT OR TYPE.

Amount Received

Why is a Certified Copy being requested?
☐ School/Sports ☐ Genealogy ☐ Medicare
☐ Social Security ID Card ☐ Welfare ☐ Veteran Benefits
☐ Passport ☐ Soc. Sec. Disability ☐ Other (specify)
☐ Driver License ☐ Other Soc. Sec. Benefits _____

Method of Payment
☐ Check ☐ Cash
☐ Money Order

Fee Due

▼ **FILL IN ONLY IF YOU WANT A BIRTH RECORD** ▼ | No. Copies Requested

| Amount Refunded | Date Refunded |

Full Name of Child at Time of Birth

Received By

Place of Birth (City, Town or Township) | County

Enclosures
☐ REG-34 ☐ REG-36 ☐ REG-37 ☐ REG-38 ☐ X
☐ REG-30 ☐ REG-40 ☐ REG-41 ☐ C

Date of Birth | Name of Hospital, If Any

Father's Name

SEARCH UNIT

Mother's Maiden Name

First Search

If Child's Name was Changed, Indicate New Name and How it was changed

REG-30

Alphabetical Second Check

▼ **FILL IN IF YOU WANT A MARRIAGE RECORD** ▼ | No. Copies Requested

File Date on Record

Name of Husband

PROCESSING UNIT

Maiden Name of Wife

Places

Place of Marriage (City, Township) | County

W W

Date of Marriage or Close Approximation

Late Months

Second Check

FOR ANY DEATH RECORD BEFORE 1901, A SEARCH CANNOT
BE MADE UNLESS YOU CAN NAME THE COUNTY WHERE THE
EVENT TOOK PLACE.

CORRESPONDENCE/RECEPTION UNIT

▼ **FILL IN ONLY IF YOU WANT A DEATH RECORD** ▼ | No. Copies Requested

REG-L7

Name of Deceased | Date of Death

Hospital Records

Place of Death (City, Town, Township, County) | Age at Death

REG-28

Residence if Different from Place of Death

Comments

Father's Name

Mother's Maiden Name

Address your envelope to:

STATE REGISTRAR - SEARCH UNIT
NEW JERSEY STATE DEPARTMENT OF HEALTH
CN 360, TRENTON, NJ 08625

COMPLETE SECTION BELOW - TYPE OR PRINT CLEARLY!
This will be used as a mailing label when we send the results of the search.

Name

Street Address

City | State | Zip Code

Dear Applicant:

The fee you paid is correct unless either block below is checked.

☐ An additional fee of $_____ is due, since either additional years or another name was involved. Send it with this form.

☐ You are entitled to a refund check of $_____ which will be forwarded within 45 days of _____. If you have occasion to write about this matter, return this form with your letter.

—STATE REGISTRAR

H-3111

VITAL
RECORDS
REQUEST

THE BUREAU OF ARCHIVES AND HISTORY MAINTAINS ALL BIRTH, MARRIAGE AND DEATH RECORDS FROM MAY 1848 THROUGH MAY 1878. All requests for vital records information after May 1878 should be directed to: State Registrar — Search Unit, New Jersey State Department of Health, CN 360, Trenton, N. J. 08625.

THE TOTAL FEE (PAYABLE IN ADVANCE) FOR A SEARCH IS   ) FOR EACH NAME. IF BIRTH, MARRIAGE AND DEATH RECORDS ARE REQUESTED, THE TOTAL SEARCH FEE WILL BE   . IF FOUND, A TYPED TRAN-SCRIPT WILL BE FORWARDED AT NO ADDITIONAL CHARGE. FEES ARE NONREFUNDABLE, WHETHER OR NOT THE REQUESTED RECORDS ARE FOUND.

PLEASE PRINT OR TYPE

NAME OF APPLICANT	DATE OF APPLICATION	FOR STATE USE ONLY
ADDRESS	TEL. NO.	
CITY STATE	ZIP CODE	DATE RECEIVED
		DATE OF RESPONSE

MAKE CHECKS OR MONEY ORDERS PAYABLE TO NEW JERSEY GENERAL TREASURY. DO NOT SEND CASH OR STAMPS. A STAMPED, SELF-ADDRESSED ENVELOPE WILL SPEED RESPONSE.

AMOUNT RECEIVED

METHOD OF PAYMENT

☐ CHECK   ☐ MONEY ORDER   ☐ CASH

FILL IN ONLY IF YOU WANT A BIRTH RECORD

FULL NAME OF CHILD AT TIME OF BIRTH

PLACE OF BIRTH (CITY, TOWN OR TOWNSHIP)   COUNTY

DATE OF BIRTH

FATHER'S NAME

MOTHER'S MAIDEN NAME

REQUEST RETURNED BECAUSE OF:

☐ INCORRECT FUNDS   ☐ PRE-1848 REQUEST

☐ POST-1878 REQUEST   ☐ INSUFFICIENT INFORMATION

☐ NO BIRTH RECORD FOUND

☐ NO MARRIAGE RECORD FOUND

☐ NO DEATH RECORD FOUND

FILL IN ONLY IF YOU WANT A MARRIAGE RECORD

NAME OF HUSBAND

MAIDEN NAME OF WIFE

PLACE OF MARRIAGE (CITY, TOWNSHIP)

COUNTY OF MARRIAGE (REQUIRED FOR SEARCHES BETWEEN 1848-1864)

DATE OF MARRIAGE

FILL IN ONLY IF YOU WANT A DEATH RECORD

NAME OF DECEASED	DATE OF DEATH
PLACE OF DEATH (CITY, TOWN, TOWNSHIP OR COUNTY)	AGE AT DEATH
FATHER'S NAME	
MOTHER'S MAIDEN NAME	

NJDE 707-16 (2/82) B

YOUR REQUEST FOR VITAL RECORDS INFORMATION IS BEING RETURNED BECAUSE:

☐ You enclosed incorrect funds. For the number of searches requested you should remit $ _____ .

☐ There are no state vital records prior to May 1, 1848.

☐ All requests for vital records information after May 1878 should be directed to: STATE REGISTRAR — SEARCH UNIT, NEW JERSEY STATE DEPARTMENT OF HEALTH, CN 360, TRENTON, N. J. 08625.

☐ YOU SUPPLIED INSUFFICIENT INFORMATION.

☐ Requests for marriage records from 1848 to 1864 must include county in which marriage took place.

☐ Requests for death records must state approximate age of deceased.

☐ Other: _____

☐ We have not found a   ☐ Birth   ☐ Marriage   ☐ Death Record for the name _____ .

We checked the indexes for the period: _____ .

☐ We have not found a   ☐ Birth   ☐ Marriage   ☐ Death Record for the name _____ .

We checked the indexes for the period: _____ .

☐ We have not found a   ☐ Birth   ☐ Marriage   ☐ Death Record for the name _____ .

We checked the indexes for the period: _____ .

STATE OF NEW JERSEY — DEPARTMENT OF EDUCATION/Division of State Library, Archives and History/Bureau of Archives and History

Send your requests to:

New Mexico Health and Environment Department
Health Services Division
Vital Statistics Office
P.O. Box 968
Santa Fe, New Mexico 87504-0968

(505) 827-0121

Send your requests for Marriage Certificates to:

County Clerk
County Court House
(County where the Marriage License was issued)

Cost for a certified Birth Certificate	$10.00
Cost for a certified Death Certificate	$10.00

The New Mexico State Vital Statistics Office has birth and death records from 1920.

If your request is urgent you may call (505) 827-0598 and charge your certificates to your visa or mastercard. There is a $6.00 fee for this service.

Search Application for BIRTH Record

STATE OF NEW MEXICO

ENVIRONMENT Health Services Division

PLEASE PRINT or TYPE

I. BIRTH CERTIFICATE OF

FULL NAME at BIRTH

DATE of BIRTH | SEX

PLACE of BIRTH *(city, county, state)*

II. PARENTS OF PERSON NAMED ON BIRTH CERTIFICATE

FATHER'S FULL NAME

MOTHER'S FULL MAIDEN NAME

ABOVE NAMED PARENTS ARE:

FATHER: ☐ Natural ☐ Adoptive   MOTHER: ☐ Natural ☐ Adoptive

III. PERSON MAKING THIS REQUEST

YOUR NAME: | Last | First | Initial

YOUR ADDRESS: | No. and Street/P.O. Box

Town | State | Zip

IV. NUMBER AND TYPE OF COPIES WANTED and FEE(S)

I am requesting:

_____ full size copy(ies)

Number

I am enclosing the Fee(s) of: $ _____

Date of Request

LEGAL NOTICE: For the protection of the individual, certificates of birth are **NOT** open to public inspection. In order to comply with this request, State Regulations require Section V below to be completed.

WARNING: False application for a birth certificate is illegal and punishable by fine and/or imprisonment.

V. STATEMENT OF REQUESTOR

Your relationship to person named in Certificate *(e.g. parent, attorney, etc.)*

For what purpose(s) do you need the copy(ies)?

Your signature

VSB 913 Revised 4/81

Search Application for DEATH Record

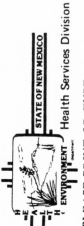

STATE OF NEW MEXICO
ENVIRONMENT DEPARTMENT **Health Services Division**

PLEASE PRINT OR TYPE

1. DEATH CERTIFICATE OF

FULL NAME of DECEASED		FULL NAME of SPOUSE *(Maiden name, if wife)*
DATE of DEATH	SEX	DECEASED's DATE of BIRTH or AGE at TIME of DEATH
PLACE of DEATH *(city, county, state)*		MORTUARY in CHARGE of FINAL ARRANGEMENTS

II. PERSON MAKING THIS REQUEST

YOUR NAME:	Last	First	Initial
YOUR ADDRESS:	No. and Street/P.O. Box		
	Town	State	Zip

III. NUMBER OF COPIES WANTED and FEE(S)

I am requesting:

_____ Certified copy(ies)
Number

I am enclosing the Fee(s) of: $ _____

_____
Date of Request

LEGAL NOTICE: For the protection of the individual whose name appears on the death certificate, and surviving family members, certificates of death are **NOT** open to public inspection.

WARNING: False application for a death certificate is illegal and punishable by fine and/or imprisonment.

IV. STATEMENT OF REQUESTOR

Your relationship to person named in certificate *(e.g. spouse, attorney, etc.)*	For what purpose(s) do you need the copy(ies)?
	Your signature

VSB **914** Revised 4/81

NEW YORK—
New York City

Send your requests to:

Bureau of Vital Records
New York City Department of Health
125 Worth Street
New York, New York 10013

(212) 566-8192

Send your requests for Marriage Certificates to:

City Clerk
(Borough where the Marriage License was issued)

Cost for a certified Birth Certificate	$5.00
Cost for a certified Death Certificate	$5.00
Cost for a duplicate copy, when ordered at the same time	$5.00

The Bureau has birth records from January 1, 1899 and death records from January 1, 1920. Please include a self-addressed stamped envelope with your request. The Municipal Archives, Department of Records and Information Services, 31 Chambers Street, New York, New York 10007, (212) 566-5292, has birth records prior to 1909, marriage records prior to 1865, and death records prior to 1929.

If your request is urgent you may call and charge your certificates to your visa or mastercard. There is a $5.00 fee for this service. Call (212) 566-6402.

THE CITY OF NEW YORK- DEPARTMENT OF HEALTH

BUREAU OF VITAL RECORDS
125 Worth Street
New York, N.Y. 10013

APPLICATION FOR A BIRTH RECORD

(Print All Items Clearly)

LAST NAME ON BIRTH RECORD	FIRST NAME	☐ FEMALE ☐ MALE

DATE OF BIRTH Month Day Year	PLACE OF BIRTH (NAME OF HOSPITAL, OR IF AT HOME, NO. AND STREET)	BOROUGH OF BIRTH

MOTHER'S MAIDEN NAME (Name Before Marriage) FIRST LAST	CERTIFICATE NUMBER IF KNOWN

FATHER'S NAME FIRST LAST	*For Office Use Only*

NO. OF COPIES	YOUR RELATIONSHIP TO PERSON NAMED ON BIRTH RECORD, IF SELF, STATE "SELF"	
	FOR WHAT PURPOSE ARE YOU GOING TO USE THIS BIRTH RECORD	

NOTE: Copy of a birth record can be issued only to persons to whom the record of birth relates, if of age, or a parent or other lawful representative. IF THIS REQUEST IS NOT FOR YOUR OWN BIRTH RECORD OR THAT OF YOUR CHILD, NOTARIZED AUTHORIZATION FROM THE PARENT OR THE PERSON NAMED ON THE CERTIFICATE MUST BE PRESENTED WITH THIS APPLICATION.

Section 3.19, New York City Health Code provides, in part:". . . no person shall make a false, untrue or misleading statement or forge the signature of another on a certificate, application, registration, report or other document required to be prepared pursuant to this Code."
Section 558 (d) of the New York City Charter provides that any violation of the Health Code shall be treated and punished as a misdemeanor.

SIGN YOUR NAME AND ADDRESS BELOW

NAME		
ADDRESS		
CITY	STATE	ZIP CODE

FEES

SEARCH FOR TWO CONSECUTIVE YEARS AND ONE COPY OR A CERTIFIED "NOT FOUND STATEMENT" ....
EACH ADDITIONAL COPY REQUESTED..
EACH EXTRA YEAR SEARCHED (WITH THIS APPLICATION)..
      1. Make check or money order payable to: Department of Health, N.Y.C.
      2. If from a foreign country, send an international money order or a check drawn on a U.S. bank.
      3. Stamps or foreign currency will not be accepted. **CASH NOT ACCEPTED BY MAIL.**

NOTE: PLEASE ATTACH A STAMPED SELF-ADDRESSED ENVELOPE.

FOR OFFICE USE ONLY

SEARCH ▶ RESULTS	REPORTED BY ☐ CRT ☐ MANUAL INITIAL ▶	CERTIFICATE NUMBER	LAST NAME - 4 LETTERS	DATE OF BIRTH
READING DATE		DATE ISSUED: BY MAIL		DATE ISSUED: IN PERSON

VR-67 (Rev. 10/82)

THE CITY OF NEW YORK - OFFICE OF THE CITY CLERK
MARRIAGE LICENSE BUREAU

REQUEST FOR A SEARCH OF A MARRIAGE LICENSE ISSUED IN ONE OF THE FIVE BOROUGHS OF
THE CITY OF NEW YORK AND A TRANSCRIPT OF SUCH MARRIAGE LICENSE

NOTE: A search for and or transcript of a marriage record will be issued only to
the person to whom the record of marriage relates, parents, children or other
lawful representative. If this record is not for your own marriage, proper written
authorization from the couple whose names appear on the record must be presented
with this application. You must also indicate a reason why a search and transcript
is needed. Attorneys, upon your own stationery, should state which party or parties
you represent and the nature of any pending action.

HOW TO OBTAIN A SEARCH AND MARRIAGE LICENSE TRANSCRIPT

1) RECORDS AVAILABLE AND WHERE TO MAIL YOUR REQUEST

Applications should be sent to: (Choose the Borough Office based on the following)

FOR RECORDS FROM   MAIL TO

* May 1943 to present: Borough where the couple obtained the license
* 1908 to May 1943:   Borough where the BRIDE resided before marriage
* 1866 to present: Borough where the couple was married

EXISTING RECORDS AVAILABLE   BOROUGH OFFICE ADDRESSES
Manhattan - 1866 to present - Municipal Bldg. New York, N.Y. 10007
Brooklyn - 1866 to present - Municipal Bldg. Brooklyn, N.Y. 11201
Queens   - 1881 to present - 120-55 Queens Blvd., Kew Gardens, N.Y. 11424
Bronx   - 1899 to present - 1780 Grand Concourse, Bronx, N.Y. 10457
Staten Island - 1898 to present - Borough Hall, St. George, Staten Island, N.Y. 10301

(LOWER LEFT-HAND CORNER OF ENVELOPE: Attention - Marriage Records)

2) FEE SCHEDULE: ALL FEES ARE PAYABLE IN ADVANCE - Fee must be paid by Certified
Check, Postal, Bank or International Money Order, payable to CITY CLERK OF NEW YORK.
Checks from foreign countries must be drawn on an American Bank. DO NOT SEND CASH
OR STAMPS.

3) VETERANS: You may obtain verification free upon surrendering the official letter
              from the Veterans Administration or State Division of Veterans Affairs.
              This letter must be an original and specifically requesting marriage
              information. This letter will not be returned to you.

CHECK FEE SCHEDULE   TODAY'S DATE: _____

Date of Marriage Ceremony: month day year	Borough where the license was issued from:
If uncertain, specify 3 years you want searched:	
Full Name of GROOM:	
Full MAIDEN Name of BRIDE:	
If woman was previously married, give FAMILY name of former HUSBAND:	
Reason search and transcript are needed:	How many copies do you need:
Name of person requesting search:	Your relationship to Bride & Groom:
Street Address City State Zip	

DO NOT WRITE BELOW - THIS SPACE FOR OFFICE USE

LICENSE
NUMBER _____ / _____   Searched
by_____   TYPE OF
CERTIF. _____

CERTIF NO. _____

Receipt No._____ Amount-$_____ Typist_____ Mailed_____

MICROFILM CARTRIDGE NUMBER _____ / _____ / _____

DATE REQUEST WAS RECEIVED_____   AMOUNT OF
MONEY RECEIVED _____

NO RECORD ( ) AMOUNT OF MONEY REFUNDED-$_____   RECEIPT
NUMBER_____ MAILED_____

THIS IS TO CERTIFY THAT_____

RESIDING AT_____ BORN

AT_____ AND _____

RESIDING AT_____ BORN

AT_____ WERE MARRIED ON _____

AT_____ BY _____

GROOM'S PARENTS:_____

BRIDE'S PARENTS:_____

WITNESSES:_____

PREVIOUS MARRIAGES:_____

REMARKS:_____

BUREAU OF VITAL RECORDS

125 WORTH STREET

NEW YORK, NEW YORK 10013

APPLICATION FOR A COPY OF A DEATH RECORD

PRINT ALL ITEMS CLEARLY

1. LAST NAME AT TIME OF DEATH	2. FIRST NAME	2A. ☐ FEMALE ☐ MALE

3. DATE OF DEATH Month Day Year	4. PLACE OF DEATH	5. BOROUGH	6. AGE

7. NO. OF COPIES	8. SPOUSE'S NAME	9. OCCUPATION OF THE DECEASED

10. FATHER'S NAME

11. BURIAL PERMIT NUMBER IF KNOWN

12. MOTHER'S NAME (Name Before Marriage)

(For Office Use Only)

13. FOR WHAT PURPOSE ARE YOU GOING TO USE THIS CERTIFICATE

NOTE: Section 205.07 of the Health Code provides, in part:" . . . The confidential medical report of death shall not be subject to subpoena or to inspection." Therefore, copies of the medical report of death cannot be issued.

SIGN YOUR NAME AND ADDRESS BELOW

NAME

ADDRESS

CITY	STATE	ZIP CODE

INFORMATION: APPLICATION SHOULD BE MADE IN PERSON OR BY MAIL TO ABOVE BUREAU.

NOTE: 1. CASH NOT ACCEPTED BY MAIL

2. PLEASE ATTACH A STAMPED SELF-ADDRESSED ENVELOPE.

FEES

SEARCH FOR TWO CONSECUTIVE YEARS AND ONE COPY..

EACH ADDITIONAL COPY REQUESTED ....

EACH EXTRA YEAR SEARCHED (WITH THIS APPLICATION) ....

IF RECORD IS NOT ON FILE, A CERTIFIED "NOT FOUND STATEMENT" WILL BE ISSUED.

1. Make check or money order payable to: Department of Health, N.Y.C.

2. If from a foreign country, send an international money order or a check drawn on a U.S. bank.

3. Stamps or foreign currency will not be accepted.

MUNICIPAL ARCHIVES
Department of Records and Information Services

31 Chambers Street
New York, N.Y. 10007

(212) 566-5292
IDILIO GRACIA PENA, *Director*

APPLICATION FOR A COPY OF A BIRTH RECORD

	OFFICE USE ONLY
FEES **DO NOT SEND CASH** Stamped, self–addressed envelope MUST be attached. Make check or money order payable to: NYC DEPARTMENT OF RECORDS AND INFORMATION SERVICES Standard fee for the issuance of a copy of a certificate based on a search of records when name, year and borough are accurately given. For each additional year to be searched. For each additional borough to be searched. For each additional copy of a certificate.	

PLEASE PRINT OR TYPE

Last name at time of birth	First name

Date of birth/Year(s) to be searched

Month	Day	Year(s)

Place of birth, please specify borough(s) to be searched

Father's name, if known

Mother's name, if known

Your relationship to person named above	No. copies requested

Your name, please print	Signature

Address

City	State	Zip Code

The City of New York

MUNICIPAL ARCHIVES
Department of Records and Information Services

31 Chambers Street
New York, N.Y. 10007

(212) 566-5292
IDILIO GRACIA PENA, *Director*

APPLICATION FOR A COPY OF A MARRIAGE RECORD.

	OFFICE USE ONLY
FEES DO NOT SEND CASH Stamped, self-addressed envelope MUST be attached. Make check or money order payable to: 　　NYC DEPARTMENT OF RECORDS AND 　　INFORMATION SERVICES 　　Standard fee for the issuance of a copy of 　　**a record based on a search of records** 　　when name, year and borough are accurately given. 　　For each additional year to be searched. 　　For each additional borough to be searched. 　　For each additional copy of a record.	

PLEASE PRINT OR TYPE:

Last name of Groom	First name of Groom
Last name of Bride (Maiden name)	First name of Bride

Date of marriage.		
Month	Day	Year(S)

Place of marriage, please specify borough(s) to be searched

Your relationship to people named above	No. copies requested

Your name, please print	Signature

Address

City	State	Zip Code

MA-25(8-85)

MUNICIPAL ARCHIVES
Department of Records and Information Services

31 Chambers Street
New York, N.Y. 10007

(212) 566-5292
IDILIO GRACIA PENA, *Director*

APPLICATION FOR A COPY OF A DEATH RECORD

	OFFICE USE ONLY
FEES	

DO NOT SEND CASH

Stamped, self-addressed envelope MUST be attached.

Make check or money order payable to:

    NYC DEPARTMENT OF RECORDS AND
    INFORMATION SERVICES

    Standard fee for the issuance of a copy of
    a certificate based on a search of records
    when name, year and borough are accurately given.

    For each additional year to be searched.
    For each additional borough to be searched.
    For each additional copy of a certificate.

PLEASE PRINT OR TYPE:

Last name at time of death	First name	Middle name

Age at death	Date of death/Year(s) to be searched	Cemetery, if known

Place of death, please specify borough(s) to be searched

Father's name, if known

Mother's name, if known

For what purpose will this record be used	No. copies requested

Your name, please print	Signature

Address

City	State	Zip Code

MA-23(5-85)

NEW YORK—
New York State

Send your requests to:

Bureau of Vital Records
New York State Department of Health
Tower Building
Empire State Plaza
Albany, New York 12237

(518) 474-3077

Cost for a certified Birth Certificate	$5.00
Cost for a certified Marriage Certificate	$5.00
Cost for a certified Death Certificate	$5.00
Cost for a duplicate copy, when ordered at the same time	$5.00

The State Bureau of Vital Records has records of births and deaths except those that occurred in New York City (See p. 105) or those that occurred in Albany, Buffalo or Yonkers prior to 1914. For these 3 cities write to the Registrar of Vital Statistics in each city.

NEW YORK STATE DEPARTMENT OF HEALTH
Bureau of Vital Records
Albany, N.Y. 12237

APPLICATION FOR A COPY OF A BIRTH RECORD

PLEASE PRINT OR TYPE

Make money order or check payable to NEW YORK STATE DEPARTMENT OF HEALTH. Please do not end csash or stamps.

No fee is charged for a copy of a record to be used for school entrance, first working papers, or for eligibility determination for social welfare and veterans' benefits.

NAME (First) (Middle) (Last)	DATE OF BIRTH OR PERIOD TO BE COVERED BY SEARCH		
PLACE OF BIRTH — Hospital (if not hospital. Give street & number)	(Village, town or city)		(County)
FATHER (First) (Middle) (Last)	MAIDEN NAME OF MOTHER	(First) (Middle) (Last)	
NUMBER OF COPIES DESIRED	ENTER BIRTH NO. IF KNOWN	ENTER LOCAL REGISTRATION NO., IF KNOWN	

PURPOSE FOR WHICH RECORD IS REQUIRED CHECK ONE

☐ Passport ☐ Working Papers ☐ Welfare Assistance

☐ Social Security ☐ School Entrance ☐ Veteran's Benefits

☐ Retirement ☐ Driver's License ☐ Court Proceeding

☐ Employment ☐ Marriage License ☐ Entrance Into Armed Forces

☐ Other (specify) _____

What is your relationship to person whose record is required? If self, state "self" _____

If attorney, give name and relationship of your client to person whose record is required _____

Signature of Applicant _____

Address of Applicant _____

Date _____

Please print name and address where record should be sent

Name _____

Address _____

City _____ State _____

VS-34B (Rev. 3/75) (5B1-47)

NEW YORK STATE DEPARTMENT OF HEALTH
Bureau of Vital Records
Albany, N.Y.
APPLICATION FOR SEARCH OF MARRIAGE RECORDS

TYPE OF RECORD DESIRED (Check One)

Search and Certification ☐

A Certification, an abstract from the marriage record issued under the seal of the Department, includes the names of the contracting parties, their residences at the time the license was issued as well as date and place of birth of the bride and groom.

A Certification may be used as proof that a marriage occurred.

Search and Certified Copy ☐

A certified Transcript includes all of the items of information occurring on the original record of the marriage.

A Certified Transcript may be needed where proof of parentage and certain other detailed information may be required such as: passports, veterans' benefits, court proceedings, or settlement of an estate.

FEES: Make money order or check payable to New York State Department of Health. Please do not send cash or stamps. There is no fee for a record to be used for eligibility determination for social welfare or veterans' benefits.

PLEASE PRINT OR TYPE

NAME OF GROOM	(First)	(Middle)	(Last)	MAIDEN NAME OF BRIDE	(First)	(Middle)	(Last)
GROOM'S AGE OR DATE OF BIRTH	(Month)	(Day)	(Year)	BRIDE'S AGE OR DATE OF BIRTH	(Month)	(Day)	(Year)
RESIDENCE OF GROOM	(County)		(State)	RESIDENCE OF BRIDE	(County)		(State)
DATE OF MARRIAGE OR PERIOD COVERED BY SEARCH				IF BRIDE PREVIOUSLY MARRIED STATE NAME USED AT THAT TIME			
PLACE WHERE LICENSE WAS ISSUED				PLACE WHERE MARRIAGE WAS PERFORMED			

For what purpose is information required _____

What is your relationship to person whose record is requested? If self, state "self" _____

In what capacity are you acting _____

If attorney: Name and relationship of your client to persons whose marriage record is required _____

Signature of Applicant _____

Address of Applicant _____

Date _____

Please print name and address where record is to be sent.

Name _____

Address _____

City _____ State _____

VS-34M (rev. 10/71)

Bureau of Vital Records
Albany, N.Y.

APPLICATION FOR SEARCH OF DEATH RECORDS

TYPE OF RECORD DESIRED (Check One)

Search and Certification ☐

A Certification, an abstract from the death certificate issued under seal of the Department, includes the name, date and place of death.

A Certification may be used as proof that the event occurred.

Search and Certified Copy ☐

A Certified Copy, a photostatic copy of the original death certificate, includes all of the information found on the original death certificate.

A Certified Copy may be required where proof of parentage and certain other detailed information may be necessary such as: veterans' benefits, court proceedings, or settlement of an estate.

FEES: Make money order or check payable to New York State Department of Health. Please do not send cash or stamps. No fee is charged for a search, certification or certified copy of a record to be used for eligibility determination for social welfare and veterans' benefits.

PLEASE PRINT OR TYPE

DEATH RECORD OF (First) (Middle) (Last)	DATE OF DEATH OR PERIOD TO BE COVERED BY SEARCH
PLACE OF DEATH (Name of Hospital or Street Address)	(Village, Town or City) (County)
SOCIAL SECURITY NUMBER OF DECEASED	DATE OF BIRTH OF DECEASED (Month) (Day) (Year) / AGE AT DEATH
NAME OF FATHER OF DECEASED (First) (Middle) (Last)	MAIDEN NAME OF MOTHER OF DECEASED (First) (Middle) (Last)
PURPOSE FOR WHICH RECORD IS REQUIRED	

What was your relationship to deceased? _____

In what capacity are you acting? _____

If attorney: Name and Relationship of your client to deceased: _____

Signature of Applicant _____

Address of Applicant _____

Date _____

Please print name and address where record should be sent:

Name _____

Address _____

City _____ State _____

NORTH CAROLINA

Send your requests to:

North Carolina Department of Human Resources
Division of Health Services
Vital Records Branch
P.O. Box 2091
Raleigh, North Carolina 27602-2091

(919) 733-3526

Cost for a certified Birth Certificate	$5.00
Cost for a certified Marriage Certificate	$5.00
Cost for a certified Death Certificate	$5.00

The North Carolina Division of Health Services has birth records from October 1, 1913, marriage records from January 1, 1962, and death records from January 1, 1930.

REQUEST FOR CERTIFICATE OF BIRTH

	First	Middle	Last	Race

NAME AT
BIRTH

	Month	Day	Year	Age

DATE OF
BIRTH

	City	County	State

PLACE OF
BIRTH

FATHER'S
FULL NAME

MOTHER'S FULL
MAIDEN NAME

SIGNATURE:

MAILING ADDRESS:

ZIP CODE:

YOUR RELATIONSHIP
TO PERSON NAMED:

CERTIFICATE NEEDED FOR	No. Copies:
	Amount: $

THE FEE FOR EACH COPY OR FOR CONDUCTING A SEARCH
WHEN NO RECORD IS FOUND IS| PLEASE MAKE CHECK
OR MONEY ORDER PAYABLE TO VITAL RECORDS BRANCH.

FORWARD APPLICATION   VITAL RECORDS BRANCH
AND FEES TO: P. O. BOX 2091
                         RALEIGH, N. C. 27602

SECTION BELOW
FOR OFFICE USE ONLY

No. Copies _____

1st Search _____

2nd Search _____

Delays _____

Date Mailed _____

Vol. & Page _____

DHS 1215 (Revised 10/85)
Vital Records

NC Department of Human Resources
Division of Health Services

PLEASE PRINT — DO NOT WRITE

GROOM

FIRST   MIDDLE   LAST

DATE OF MARRIAGE

MONTH   DAY   YEAR

PLACE OF MARRIAGE

CITY   COUNTY   STATE

IF FOR MARRIAGE
FULL MAIDEN NAME OF BRIDE

IF FOR MARRIAGE
NAME OF MINISTER OR MAGISTRATE

IF FOR DIVORCE
FULL NAME OF DEFENDANT

CERTIFICATE
NEEDED FOR

What is your relationship
to the person named on
the certificate?

NAME, ADDRESS
AND ZIP CODE
OF APPLICANT

PHS 2103 - 4/71

SECTION BELOW
FOR OFFICE USE ONLY

No Copies

1st Search

2nd Search

Date Mailed

Vol. & Page

NC Department of Human Resources
Division of Health Services

NAME OF DECEASED

FIRST   MIDDLE   LAST   RACE

DATE OF DEATH

MONTH   DAY   YEAR   AGE

PLACE OF DEATH

CITY   COUNTY   STATE

NAME OF WIFE OR HUSBAND

NAME OF FATHER

NAME OF MOTHER

NAME & ADDRESS OF FUNERAL HOME

What is your relationship to the person named on the certificate?

NAME, ADDRESS AND ZIP CODE OF APPLICANT

DHS FORM 1293 REV. 9/75
VITAL RECORDS

SECTION BELOW FOR OFFICE USE ONLY

No Copies _____

1st Search _____

2nd Search _____

Date Mailed _____

Vol. & Page _____

NC Department of Human Resources
Division of Health Services

NORTH DAKOTA

Send your requests to:

North Dakota State Department of Health
Division of Health Statistics and Vital Records
State Capitol
Bismarck, North Dakota 58505

(701) 224-4508

Cost for a certified Birth Certificate	$7.00
Additional copy of Birth Certificate	$4.00
Cost for a certified Marriage Certificate	$5.00
Cost for a certified Death Certificate	$5.00

The North Dakota State Department of Health has birth and death records from July 1, 1893 and marriage records from July 1, 1925.

If your request is urgent you may call and charge your certificates to your visa or mastercard. There is a $5.00 fee for this service.

REQUEST FOR COPY OF BIRTH CERTIFICATE

Please Print

FULL NAME AT BIRTH				
DATE OF BIRTH	(month)	(day)	(year)	SEX
PLACE OF BIRTH	(city or township)		(county)	
RESIDENCE OF PARENTS AT TIME OF THIS BIRTH				
FULL NAME OF FATHER	(first)	(middle)	(last)	
FULL NAME OF MOTHER	(first)	(middle)	(maiden)	

ORDER OF BIRTH (1st child, 2nd, etc.)   IS THIS CERTIFICATE FOR AN ADOPTED CHILD? Yes____ No____

FOR WHAT PURPOSE IS THIS COPY REQUESTED?   Enclosed is $___ for ___ certified copies. (See fee schedule below)

IF NOT REQUESTING YOUR OWN CERTIFICATE, WHAT IS YOUR RELATIONSHIP TO THE ABOVE-NAMED PERSON?   **Type of Copy Desired** ( ) Paper Copy ( ) Plastic Birth Card

SIGNATURE OF PERSON MAKING THIS REQUEST

PRINTED NAME

ADDRESS

CITY	STATE	ZIP CODE	DAYTIME TELEPHONE NUMBER (area code and seven digits)

IF COPY TO BE MAILED ELSEWHERE

NAME

ADDRESS	CITY	STATE	ZIP CODE

The above information is necessary to properly identify and locate the correct birth certificate. Please enter full information.

Birth certificates are by law confidential. Copies or information are to be furnished only to persons having a direct and tangible interest — the registrant, parent or guardian, legal representative, or on court order.

The fee for one certified copy is ___ Additional copies of the same certificate issued at the same time are ___ each. (Two dollars of this fee is used to support the Children's Trust Fund, a state fund for aiding in the prevention of child abuse and neglect.)

NOTE: Make all checks or money orders payable to "NORTH DAKOTA STATE DEPARTMENT OF HEALTH." Cash is sent at your own risk!

THIS PORTION FOR VITAL RECORD'S OFFICE USE ONLY

Date:_____

Telephone___ Client___ Mail___ Fee Received_____

Searcher:_____

State File No. 133-_____

Number/Type Copies Issued_____

REMARKS:

Mail request with fee to:

**NORTH DAKOTA STATE DEPARTMENT OF HEALTH
VITAL RECORDS
STATE CAPITOL
BISMARCK, ND 58505**

SFN 814

REQUEST FOR COPY OF MARRIAGE RECORD

Please Print

FULL NAME OF GROOM	FULL MAIDEN NAME OF BRIDE
RESIDENCE OF GROOM AT MARRIAGE	RESIDENCE OF BRIDE AT MARRIAGE

DATE OF MARRIAGE (Month) (Day) (Year)	COUNTY WHERE LICENSE ISSUED

PLACE WHERE MARRIED (City)	(County)

FOR WHAT PURPOSE IS COPY NEEDED	YOUR RELATIONSHIP TO GROOM/BRIDE (e.g. self, parent, attorney — specify)

SIGNATURE OF APPLICANT

STREET ADDRESS OR BOX NUMBER

CITY AND STATE	ZIP CODE	Enclosed is $_____ for _____ certified copies.

Original Licenses and Certificates of Marriage are filed in the office of the **COUNTY JUDGE** of the **COUNTY WHERE THE LICENSE WAS ISSUED.** It is recommended that requests for certified copies be directed to the custodian of the <u>original</u> record as follows:

County Judge
County Where License Was Issued
County Seat

See reverse side of this form for a list of the North Dakota counties, respective county seats, and zip codes.

* *

Since July 1, 1925, copies of Licenses and Certificates of Marriage have been forwarded to the State Registrar for statistical purposes and for maintaining a state-wide index. The state office is also authorized to issue certified copies. For marriages which have occurred **since July 1, 1925,** you may secure copies from the County Judge (as noted above) or from address listed below!

THIS PORTION FOR VITAL RECORD'S OFFICE USE ONLY

Date:_____

Telephone_____ Client_____ Mail_____

Searcher:_____

State File No. 133—_____

Number/Type Copies Issued_____

REMARKS:

Mail request with fee to:

NORTH DAKOTA STATE DEPARTMENT OF HEALTH
VITAL RECORDS
STATE CAPITOL
BISMARCK, ND 58505

REQUEST FOR COPY OF DEATH CERTIFICATE

Please Print

FULL NAME OF DECEASED					SEX
DATE OF DEATH (Month)	(Day)		(Year)	SPOUSE'S NAME	
PLACE OF DEATH (Hospital)		(City)		(County)	
WHAT IS YOUR RELATIONSHIP TO THE DECEASED?				FUNERAL HOME	
FOR WHAT PURPOSE IS THIS COPY REQUESTED?				Enclosed is $_____ for _____ certified copies.	

SIGNATURE OF PERSON MAKING THIS REQUEST
PRINTED NAME

ADDRESS	CITY	STATE	ZIP CODE

TELEPHONE NO. (area code and seven digits)
IF COPY TO BE MAILED ELSEWHERE
NAME

ADDRESS	CITY	STATE	ZIP CODE

The above information is necessary to properly identify and locate the correct death certificate. Please enter full information.

Death certificates are by law confidential, and copies or information are to be furnished only to persons having a direct and tangible interest — a parent, a member of the immediate family, a legal representative, or on court order. Be sure to state your relationship to the deceased and the purpose for which the copy is needed.

NOTE: Make all checks or money orders payable to the "NORTH DAKOTA STATE DEPARTMENT OF HEALTH." Cash is sent at your own risk!

THIS PORTION FOR VITAL RECORD'S OFFICE USE ONLY

Date: _____

Telephone_____ Client_____ Mail_____

Searcher: _____

State File No. 133—_____

Number/Type Copies Issued_____

REMARKS:

Mail request with fee to:

NORTH DAKOTA STATE DEPARTMENT OF HEALTH
VITAL RECORDS
STATE CAPITOL
BISMARCK, ND 58505

Send your requests to:

Ohio State Department of Health
Division of Vital Statistics
Ohio Departments Building, Room G-20
65 South Front Street
Columbus, Ohio 43266-0333

(614) 466-2533

Send your requests for Marriage Certificates to:

Probate Judge
County Probate Court
(County where the Marriage License was issued)

Cost for a certified Birth Certificate	$7.00
Cost for a certified Death Certificate	$7.00

The Ohio State Department of Health has birth and death records from December 20, 1908. If you simply require an uncertified copy of the birth or death certificate the cost is $1.10 per copy.

STATE OF OHIO

DEPARTMENT OF HEALTH

DIVISION OF VITAL STATISTICS

COLUMBUS, OHIO 43266-0333

DO NOT WRITE IN THIS SPACE

DATE OF RECEIPT

AMOUNT | NO. OF COPIES

VOLUME NO.

CERTIFICATE NO.

APPLICATION FOR CERTIFIED COPY OF BIRTH CERTIFICATE

IMPORTANT

(ENCLOSE CHECK OR MONEY ORDER — DO NOT SEND CASH)

TO BE PRINTED

INFORMATION ABOUT PERSON WHOSE BIRTH CERTIFICATE IS REQUESTED

	FIRST	MIDDLE	LAST
Full Name at Birth			

	MONTH	DAY	YEAR	AGE (AT LAST BIRTHDAY)
Date of Birth				

	COUNTY	CITY, VILLAGE OR TOWNSHIP	STATE OHIO
Place of Birth			

	FIRST	MIDDLE	LAST
Full name of Father			

	FIRST	MIDDLE	LAST (MAIDEN)
Mother's maiden name (name before marriage)			

Name of person making application	Date	Telephone number

Present Address - Street and Number or Rural Route

Amount Enclosed $ _____

City or Village	State	☐ Check ☐ Money Order

To your knowledge has a copy of this record been obtained before?   ☐ Yes   ☐ No   ☐ Unknown

DO NOT DETACH

Print name and address of person to whom certificate(s) is (are) to be mailed in the space below —— this is a mailing insert and will be used to mail the certified copy which you have requested. When the above application and the name and address in the section below have been completed please send the entire form to:

⬇

_____
NAME

_____
STREET NO. & NAME

_____
CITY ------- STATE   ZIP CODE

OHIO DEPARTMENT OF HEALTH

Division of Vital Statistics

65 South Front Street

Columbus, Ohio 43266-0333

HEA 2709 (Rev. 7/85)   4

5132 06

DO NOT WRITE IN THIS SPACE

STATE OF OHIO

DEPARTMENT OF HEALTH

DIVISION OF VITAL STATISTICS

COLUMBUS, OHIO 43266-0333

DATE OF RECEIPT	
AMOUNT	NO. OF COPIES
VOLUME NO.	
CERTIFICATE NO.	

APPLICATION FOR CERTIFIED COPY OF DEATH CERTIFICATE

IMPORTANT

(ENCLOSE CHECK OR MONEY ORDER — DO NOT SEND CASH)

TO BE PRINTED

INFORMATION ABOUT PERSON WHOSE DEATH CERTIFICATE IS REQUESTED

Name of Deceased _____

Date of Death _____

Place of Death

County _____

City or Village _____

Township _____

Funeral Director _____

Address of Funeral Director

Applicant's Signature _____

Amount Enclosed $ _____

☐ Check   ☐ Money Order

Street and Number _____ City ········ State _____ Zip Code _____

DO NOT DETACH

Print name and address of person to whom certificate(s) is (are) to be mailed in the space below — — this is a mailing insert and will be used to mail the certified copy which you have requested. When the above application and the name and address in the section below have been completed please send the entire form to:

NAME _____

STREET NO. & NAME _____

CITY ········ STATE _____ ZIP CODE _____

OHIO DEPARTMENT OF HEALTH

Division of Vital Statistics

Room G-20

65 South Front Street

Columbus, Ohio 43266-0333

HEA 2712 (Rev. 7/85)

V.S.
5161.

OKLAHOMA

Send your requests to:

> Division of Vital Records
> Oklahoma State Department of Health
> N.E. 10th and Stonewall
> P.O. Box 53551
> Oklahoma City, Oklahoma 73152

(405) 271-4040

Send your requests for Marriage Certificates to:

> County Clerk
> County Court House
> (County where the Marriage License was issued)

Cost for a certified Birth Certificate	$5.00
Cost for a certified Death Certificate	$5.00

The Oklahoma State Department of Health has birth and death records from October 1908. The Department, at this time, provides an application form for death certificates only.

Disvision of Vital Records, Oklahoma State Department of Health

APPLICATION FOR SEARCH AND CERTIFIED COPY OF DEATH CERTIFICATE

Facts Concerning This Death

Full name of deceased _____ Race _____

Date of
death _____ Place of
death _____ , OKLAHOMA
      (Mo.)   (Day)   (Year)   (County)   (City)

Check box if death was stillbirth or fetal death ☐

Funeral director
in charge _____ Address _____

Purpose for which this copy is needed _____

Signature of person
making this application _____ Date of
application _____

PLEASE PRINT CORRECT MAILING ADDRESS BELOW:

Number of copies
wanted _____

_____
(Name)

Fee enclosed $ _____

_____
(Street address)

ENCLOSE A STAMPED,
SELF-ADDRESSED
ENVELOPE WITH THIS
APPLICATION

_____
(City)   (State)

Request for a search of the records for a death certificate of any person who died in the State of Oklahoma should be submitted on this blank along with the required fee of   If the death certificate is on file a certified copy will be mailed.

The information requested above should be filled in carefully and accurately. It is the minimum needed to make a thorough search for a death record.

Send   dollars   in cash, money order or check for each copy desired. Cash is sent at sender's risk. Make checks or money orders payable to the State Department of Health.

A copy required to be submitted to the Veterans Administration or U. S. Commissioner of Pensions, in connection with a claim for military-service-connected benefits may be obtained without fee provided a signed statement is attached which sets forth these facts and requests that the copy be issued without fee. Members of the armed forces and veterans must pay regular fees for copies to be used for all other purposes.

VS 150 10-84

OREGON

Send your requests to:

Oregon State Department of Human Resources
State Health Division
Vital Statistics Section
State Office Building, Room 101
1400 S.W. 5th Avenue
P.O. Box 116
Portland, Oregon 97207-0231

(503) 229-5895

Cost for a certified Birth Certificate	$8.00
Cost for a wallet size Birth Certificate	$5.00
Cost for a certified Marriage Certificate	$8.00
Cost for a certified Death Certificate	$8.00

The Oregon Department of Human Resources has birth and death records from January 1, 1903 and marriage records from January 1, 1906.

You may call the office to order copies of certificates and charge them to your visa or mastercard. There is an additional $5.00 fee for this service.

State of Oregon
Department of Human Resources
HEALTH DIVISION

VITAL RECORDS ORDER FORM

PLEASE SPECIFY TYPE OF RECORD YOU WANT AND HOW MANY—

	How Many			How Many
BIRTH CARD			MARRIAGE	
BIRTH — Full			DIVORCE	
DEATH				

ALL RECORDS ARE   EACH

DO NOT WRITE IN THIS SPACE

OFFICE USE ONLY

TO ATTENTION OF:

CERTIFICATE #:

1. NAME ON RECORD: (First)   (Middle)   (Last)

2. NAME OF SPOUSE: (Death, marriage, divorce only)

| | | 1 | 2 |

3. DATE OF EVENT: (Month)   (Day)   (Year)   SEX

4. PLACE OF EVENT: (City)   (County)   **OREGON**

5. FATHER'S NAME:

6. MOTHER'S FIRST & MAIDEN NAME:

7. NAME OF AGENCY OR PERSON ORDERING RECORD:

8. YOUR RELATIONSHIP TO LINE 1:

9. DAYTIME PHONE NUMBER:

OFFICE USE ONLY

	FILM	
Amendment Fee	FILM (P)	
Full Issued	COMPUTER	
	INDEXES	
Card Issued	INDEX (P)	
	DF/CO	
NRL/Ref. Issued	REFUND: $	
	Excess Fee: Out/State:	
File Date	No Rec: Uncompltd:	
	CHECK: #	

PLEASE NOTE: The fee for each item requested is   If the requested record cannot be found a   search fee
must be retained as prescribed by law — ORS 432.145.

PLEASE ENCLOSE THE CORRECT FEE WITH THIS APPLICATION FORM
Make checks or money orders payable to: OREGON STATE HEALTH DIVISION

The Oregon Vital Records Unit has the following records —

Birth in Oregon since 1903	Death in Oregon since 1903
Marriage in Oregon since 1906	Divorce in Oregon since 1925

In accordance with law — ORS 432.120, in addition to having one's own record, a birth record can be furnished to the parents, guardian or respective representative. If you do not fall into one of the above categories, we will need written permission from one of the above eligible persons. The written consent must accompany return of this form. We can send the copy directly to the registrant if the address is available.

Your Mailing Address Must Be Entered Below:

NAME

STREET

CITY, STATE   ZIP

YOUR MAILING ADDRESS

Thank you for your order.

This is not a bill.

In case yours was an order for more than one person's record, the other parts of your order will be handled and sent separately.

45-13   (R-1-

PENNSYLVANIA

Send your requests to:

Pennsylvania Department of Health
Division of Vital Records
101 South Mercer Street
P.O. Box 1528
New Castle, Pennsylvania 16103

(717) 787-8552

Send your requests for Marriage Certificates to:

County Clerk
County Court House
(County where the Marriage License was issued)

Cost for a certified Birth Certificate	$4.00
Cost for a certified Death Certificate	$3.00

The Pennsylvania Department of Health has birth and death records from January 1903. Include a self-addressed stamped envelope with your request.

H105.102 REV 8-85

PENNSYLVANIA DEPARTMENT OF HEALTH
VITAL RECORDS

APPLICATION FOR CERTIFIED COPY OF BIRTH OR DEATH RECORD
RECORDS AVAILABLE FROM 1906 TO THE PRESENT

PRINT OR TYPE ALL ITEMS MUST BE COMPLETED OFFICE USE ON

INDICATE NUMBER OF COPIES	☐ BIRTH	☐ DEATH	
1. Date of Birth OR Date of Death	2. Place of Birth OR Place of Death / County / Boro/City/Twp.	File No.
3. Name at Birth OR Name at Death	4. Sex / 5. Age	Searched By
6. Father's Full Name — First / Middle / Last		Typed By
7. Mother's Maiden Name — First / Middle / Last		File Date
8. Hospital / Funeral Director		Refund Ck. No
9. REASON FOR REQUEST. THIS ITEM MUST BE COMPLETED		Date A
10. HOW ARE YOU RELATED TO THIS PERSON?		
11. Signature of Applicant (If Subject Under 18, Parent Must Sign)		
12. Mailing Address		
13. City, State, Zip Code		
14. Daytime Phone Number — Area Code: / Number:		

NOT REFUNDABLE
DO NOT SEND CASH
Make Check or Money Order Payable to VITAL RECORDS

PLEASE ENCLOSE A LEGAL-SIZE SELF-ADDRESSED STAMPED ENVELOPE FOR RETURN OF COPIES

IF ALL ITEMS ARE NOT COMPLETED, APPLICATION MAY BE REJECTED

☐ Prev. Amend.   ☐ Adopt   ☐ Affi
☐ Usage   ☐ Court Order   ☐ Is: Affi

DO NOT REMOVE THIS STUB

If birth or death occured in: Mail application to:

1) Philadelphia — Division of Vital Records, 402 City Hall Annex, Philadelphia, Pa. 19107
2) Pittsburgh — Division of Vital Records, Room 512, 300 Liberty Ave., Pittsburgh, Pa. 15222
3) Erie — Division of Vital Records, 3832 Liberty St., Erie, Pa. 16509
4) Scranton — Division of Vital Records, 100 Lackawanna Ave., Scranton, Pa. 18503

Print or type your name and address in the space below.

Name
Street
City, State, Zip Code

FOR ALL OTHER AREAS
MAIL COMPLETED APPLICATION TO:

PENNSYLVANIA DEPARTMENT OF HEALTH
DIVISION OF VITAL RECORDS
P.O. BOX 1528
NEW CASTLE, PA. 16103
or visit our public offices at
101 South Mercer Street, New Castle

RHODE ISLAND

Send your requests to:

Division of Vital Statistics
Rhode Island Department of Health
Cannon Building, Room 101
75 Davis Street
Providence, Rhode Island 02908

(401) 277-2811

Cost for a certified Birth Certificate	$5.00
Cost for a wallet size Birth Certificate	$5.00
Cost for a certified Marriage Certificate	$5.00
Cost for a certified Death Certificate	$5.00
Cost for a duplicate copy, when ordered at the same time	$3.00

The Rhode Island Division of Vital Statistics has records from 1853. Make your check payable to "General Treasurer, State of Rhode Island."

RHODE ISLAND DEPARTMENT OF HEALTH   DIVISION OF VITAL STATISTICS

APPLICATION FOR A CERTIFIED COPY OF A BIRTH RECORD

1. Please fill in the information below for the individual whose birth record you are requesting:

    FULL NAME AT BIRTH _____

    DATE OF BIRTH _____ CITY/TOWN OF BIRTH _____

    MOTHER'S FULL MAIDEN NAME _____

    FATHER'S FULL NAME _____

2. What is your relationship to the person whose record is being requested?

    _____

3. Why do you need this record? _____

    _____

4. Do you want a FULL COPY of the record or a WALLET-SIZE COPY? (A full copy is good for every purpose; a wallet-size is convenient for carrying, but may not be accepted by every agency).

    (Indicate number of copies) [   ] FULL COPY [   ] WALLET SIZE

5. YOUR SIGNATURE _____ DATE SIGNED _____

    PLEASE ALSO PRINT YOUR NAME HERE _____

    YOUR FULL MAILING ADDRESS _____

    _____

****

BELOW THIS LINE FOR OFFICE USE ONLY

State File
Number_____   Amount
                     Rec'd_____   Form of
                                         Remittance_____   Date Copy
                                                                  Sent_____

Type of Copy
Given_____   Initials of
                     Person Issuing_____   Date of Birth_____

No. of Copies____First copy   Additional copies of same record at

_____Additional years of search at   per year = _____

Delayed birth, correction, paternity, adoption or legitimation at   _____

VS 82B 7/83

RHODE ISLAND DEPARTMENT OF HEALTH   DIVISION OF VITAL STATISTICS

APPLICATION FOR A CERTIFIED COPY OF A MARRIAGE RECORD

1. Please fill in the information below for the persons whose marriage record you
   are requesting:

   FULL NAME OF GROOM_____

   FULL NAME OF BRIDE_____

   FULL MAIDEN NAME OF BRIDE (IF DIFFERENT)_____

   DATE OF MARRIAGE_____PLACE OF MARRIAGE_____

2. What is your relationship to the persons whose marriage record is being requested?

   _____

3. Why do you need this record?_____

   _____

4. YOUR SIGNATURE_____DATE SIGNED_____

   PLEASE ALSO PRINT YOUR NAME HERE_____

   YOUR FULL MAILING ADDRESS_____

   _____

****

BELOW THIS LINE FOR OFFICE USE ONLY _____

State File   Amount   Form of   Date Copy
Number_____   Rec'd $_____   Remittance_____ Sent_____

Type of copy   Initials of
given_____   person issuing_____Date of Marriage_____

No. of copies_____First copy   Additional copies of same record at

_____Additional years of search at   per year =_____

VS 82M   7/83

RHODE ISLAND DEPARTMENT OF HEALTH   DIVISION OF VITAL STATISTICS

APPLICATION FOR A CERTIFIED COPY OF A DEATH RECORD

1. Please fill in the information below for the individual whose death record you are requesting:

   FULL NAME_____

   DATE OF DEATH_____PLACE OF DEATH_____

   NAME OF SPOUSE (IF MARRIED)_____

   MOTHER'S FULL MAIDEN NAME_____

   FATHER'S FULL NAME_____

2. What is your relationship to the person whose death record is being requested?

   _____

3. Why do you need this record?_____

   _____

4. YOUR SIGNATURE_____DATE SIGNED_____

   PLEASE ALSO PRINT YOUR NAME HERE_____

   YOUR FULL MAILING ADDRESS_____

   _____

5. Number of Copies_____

****

BELOW THIS LINE FOR OFFICE USE ONLY

State File Number	Amount Rec'd $	Form of Remittance	Date Copy Sent

Type of copy given_____Initials of person issuing_____Date of death_____

No. of copies____ First copy ____Additional copies of same record at

____Additional years of search at ____per year = _____

VS 82D   7/83

SOUTH CAROLINA

Send your requests to:

South Carolina Department of Health
   and Environmental Control
Office of Vital Records & Public Health Statistics
2600 Bull Street
Columbia, South Carolina 29201

(803) 734-4830

Cost for a certified Birth Certificate	$5.00
Cost for a wallet size Birth Certificate	$5.00
Cost for a certified Marriage Certificate	$5.00
Cost for a certified Death Certificate	$5.00
Cost for a duplicate copy, when ordered at the same time	$1.00

The South Carolina Office of Vital Records has birth and death records from January 1, 1915 and marriage records from July 1, 1950.

If your request is urgent you may call and charge your certificates to your visa or mastercard. There is a charge of $19.75 for this service including the postal costs.

SOUTH CAROLINA DEPARTMENT OF HEALTH AND ENVIRONMENTAL CONTROL

OFFICE OF VITAL RECORDS & PUBLIC HEALTH STATISTICS
2600 BULL STREET
COLUMBIA, S. C. 29201

APPLICATION FOR CERTIFIED COPY OF BIRTH CERTIFICATE

INFORMATION	INSTRUCTIONS
1. Only births recorded after **January 1, 1915** in South Carolina are on file.	1. Complete all of the information sections required on this form. **PLEASE PRINT.**
2. S. C. Law requires a ____ fee for the search of a birth record. If located, a standard certification of birth will be issued. If not located, search fee is not refundable.	2. The application must be signed by **registrant, parent/guardian, or their legal representative.**
3. **WARNING: FALSE APPLICATION IS PUNISHABLE BY LAW.** (Section 44-63-161; S. C. Code of Laws, 1976, Amended, July 18, 1978.)	3. Send completed application and appropriate fee to the address at the top of this form. Checks and money orders should be made payable to Office of Vital Records.

1. FULL NAME	First Name	Middle Name	Last Name	OFFICE USE ONL
2. DATE OF BIRTH	Month	Day	Year	Year — Cert. No.
3. PLACE OF BIRTH	County	Hospital/and or city/town	State South Carolina	Search 1st ____ Date
				2nd ____ Date
4. SEX		5. RACE		

| 6. FULL NAME OF FATHER | First Name | Middle Name | Last Name | Living ☐ Deceased ☐ | Pending Sect. ____ Date C |
| 7. FULL MAIDEN NAME OF MOTHER | First Name | Middle Name | Maiden Name | Living ☐ Deceased ☐ | D |

8. WERE PARENTS MARRIED? Yes ☐ No ☐	9. NUMBER OF CHILD (1st, 2nd, etc...)	A
		L

| 10. NAME OF NEXT OLDER BROTHER OR SISTER, LIVING OR DEAD | | DATE OF BIRTH | | PR |
| 11. NAME OF NEXT YOUNGER BROTHER OR SISTER LIVING OR DEAD | | DATE OF BIRTH | | LOC |

12. HAS NAME EVER BEEN CHANGED OTHER THAN MARRIAGE? Yes ☐ No ☐	If so, what was the original name?	Final Disposition
		Issue Date

13. PURPOSE FOR WHICH THIS COPY IS REQUESTED?		Control Number(s)

FEE

14. I am enclosing $ _____ for _____ certificates as follows: **Specify Number and Type Certification**

_____ **Wallet size, short form certification** - Accepted for all purposes except to establish relationship of parent to child. Does not include parents' names. Initial certification - _____ Additional short form certification ordered at same time - _____ each.

_____ **Photocopy certification** - Issued only by the state office and only to registrant if of legal age (18 yrs.) parent/guardian or their legal representative. Initial certification - _____ Additional photocopy certification ordered at same time - _____ each.

15. WRITTEN SIGNATURE OF registrant, parent/guardian or legal representative **DO NOT PRINT**		Your relationship to registrant: Self ____ Parent ____ Guardian ____ Other (specify) _____	☐ Refund Refunded Amount $ _____

ADDRESS

PLEASE PRINT

16. NAME

17. NUMBER, P.O. BOX AND STREET

18. CITY, STATE, AND ZIP CODE

SCDHEC - 612 (Rev. 12-82)

SOUTH CAROLINA DEPARTMENT OF HEALTH AND ENVIRONMENTAL CONTROL

OFFICE OF VITAL RECORDS & PUBLIC HEALTH STATISTICS
2600 BULL STREET
COLUMBIA, S. C. 29201

APPLICATION FOR CERTIFIED COPY OF MARRIAGE RECORD

INFORMATION

1. Only marriage licenses issued **after July, 1950, in South Carolina** are on file.

2. S. C. Law requires a _____ fee for the search of a marriage record. If located, a certified copy of the marriage record will be issued. Additional copies of the same record ordered at the same time are _____ each. If not located, search fee is not refundable.

3. If the marriage occurred prior to July, 1950, or if a copy of the application is required, contact the probate judge of the county where the marriage license was issued.

INSTRUCTIONS

1. Complete all the information sections of the form. **PLEASE PRINT.**

2. An application for a certified copy of a marriage record must be **signed by one of the parties married, their adult child, or the legal representative of one of these persons. Relationship must be stated.**

3. Send completed application and appropriate fee to the address at the top of this form. Checks and money orders should be made payable to the office of Vital Records.

	First	Middle	Last		OFFICE USE ONLY
1. FULL NAME OF GROOM					
2. DATE OF BIRTH	Month	Day	Year	Race	YEAR – CERT. NO.
3. FULL NAME OF BRIDE	First	Middle	Last		
4. DATE OF OF BIRTH	Month	Day	Year	Race	PROC. DATE

5. HAS BRIDE EVER USED ANY OTHER NAME? ☐ Yes ☐ No   If so, please list: _____   DNL.   DATE

	Month	Day	Year	FINAL DISPOSITION
6. DATE OF MARRIAGE				ISSUE DATE
7. PLACE LICENSE ISSUED	City	County	State South Carolina	

8. FEE   I am enclosing a Fee of $ _____ for _____ CERTIFIED COPIES.   CONTROL NO.

9. WRITTEN SIGNATURE OF ONE OF MARRIED PARTIES, ADULT CHILDREN, OR LEGAL REPRESENTATIVE | Relationship   Self_____ Adult child_____ Legal rep_____

☐ Refund
Refunded
Amount $_____

CERTIFICATE TO BE MAILED TO: (PLEASE PRINT)

10. NAME

11. NUMBER, P. O. BOX AND STREET

12. CITY, STATE, AND ZIP CODE

SCDHEC-678 (Rev. 12-82)

SOUTH CAROLINA DEPARTMENT OF HEALTH AND ENVIRONMENTAL CONTROL

OFFICE OF VITAL RECORDS & PUBLIC HEALTH STATISTICS
2600 BULL STREET
COLUMBIA, S. C. 29201

APPLICATION FOR CERTIFIED COPY OF A DEATH RECORD

INFORMATION

1. Only deaths recorded **after January 1, 1915, in South Carolina** are on file.

2. S. C. Law requires a   fee for the search of a death record. If located, a certified copy of the death record will be issued. Additional copies of the same record ordered at the same time are   each. If not located, search fee is not refundable.

3. Verification of date and place of death will be provided if the relationship of the applicant prohibits the issuance of a certified copy. (Regulation 61-19, Section 39, Code of Laws of South Carolina, 1976)

4. WARNING: FALSE APPLICATION FOR A DEATH CERTIFICATE IS PUNISHABLE BY LAW. (Section 44-63-161, South Carolina Code of Laws, 1976, Amended, July 18, 1978)

INSTRUCTION

1. Complete all the information sections of the form. **PLEASE PRINT.**

2. An application for a certified copy of a death certificate must be **signed by a surviving relative of the deceased person or his legal representative. Relationship must be stated.**

3. Send completed application and appropriate fee to the address at the top of this form. Checks and money orders should be made payable to the Office of Vital Records.

1. FULL NAME OF DECEASED	Last Name	First Name	Middle Name and/or Maiden	OFFICE USE ONLY
2. DATE OF DEATH	Month	Day	Year	Year — Cert. No.
3. PLACE OF DEATH	Hospital/City	County	State SOUTH CAROLINA	DNL. DATE
4. SEX	5. RACE		6. AGE AT TIME OF DEATH	PROC. DATE
7. SOCIAL SECURITY NO. OF DECEASED (IF KNOWN)				
8. NAME OF FUNERAL DIRECTOR				Final Disposition
9. IF THE DECEASED WAS MARRIED; PLEASE LIST HUSBAND/WIFE			Living ☐ Dead ☐	ISSUE DATE
10. FATHER OF THE DECEASED	Last Name First Name Middle Name			CONTROL NO.
11. MOTHER OF THE DECEASED	Last Name First Name Middle Name			
12. FEE	I am enclosing a Fee of $ _____ for _____ CERTIFIED COPIES.			
13. WRITTEN SIGNATURE OF SURVIVING RELATIVE OR LEGAL REPRESENTATIVE		RELATION TO DECEASED		☐ Refund Refunded Amount $ _____

CERTIFICATE TO BE MAILED TO: (PLEASE PRINT)

14. NAME

15. NUMBER, P. O. BOX AND STREET

16. CITY, STATE, AND ZIP CODE

SCDHEC-677 (Rev. 12-82)

SOUTH DAKOTA

Send your requests to:

South Dakota Department of Health
Center for Health Statistics
Joe Foss Building
523 East Capitol
Pierre, South Dakota 57501-3182

(605) 773-3355

Cost for a certified Birth Certificate	$5.00
Cost for a certified Marriage Certificate	$5.00
Cost for a certified Death Certificate	$5.00

The South Dakota Department of Health has records from July 1905.

If your request is urgent you may call (605) 773-4961 and charge your certificates to your visa or mastercard. There is a $5.00 fee for this service.

Department of Health

Center For Health Statistics
523 East Capitol, Joe Foss Bldg.
Pierre, South Dakota 57501-3182
605/773-3355

RECEIPT #_____

DATE_____

We have received your request and fee of $_____for a certified copy of a vital record.
We require an additional fee of $_____before we can process your request. THE ADDITIONAL
FEE AND THIS COMPLETED FORM MUST BE RETURNED WITHIN 30 DAYS.

BIRTH	FULL NAME AT BIRTH OR ADOPTIVE NAME_____ DATE OF BIRTH (Month, Day & Year)_____ PLACE OF BIRTH (City & County)_____ FATHER'S FULL NAME_____ MOTHER'S FULL MAIDEN NAME_____ STATE REASON RECORD IS NEEDED_____ (Applies only to out of wedlock births) _____ (Signature of person requesting record)
DEATH	FULL NAME AT TIME OF DEATH_____ DATE OF DEATH (Month, Day & Year)_____ PLACE OF DEATH (City & County)_____
MARRIAGE	FULL NAME OF GROOM_____ FULL NAME OF BRIDE_____ DATE OF MARRIAGE (Month, Day & Year)_____
DIVORCE	FULL NAME OF HUSBAND_____ FULL NAME OF WIFE_____ DATE OF DIVORCE (Month, Day & Year)_____

PRINT OR TYPE NAME AND ADDRESS OF PERSON TO WHOM CERTIFICATE IS TO BE SENT

_____
(Name)

_____
(Street or Box)

_____
(City and State)   ZIP

HAS-0252 REV. 4-85

TENNESSEE

Send your requests to:

Tennessee State Department of Health
   and Environment
Vital Records Office
Cordell Hull Building
Nashville, Tennessee 37219-5402

(615) 741-1763

Cost for a certified Birth Certificate	$10.00
Cost for a short form Birth Certificate	$ 5.00
Cost for a certified Marriage Certificate	$10.00
Cost for a certified Death Certificate	$ 4.00

The Tennessee Office of Vital Records has birth and death records from January 1, 1914 and marriage records from July 1, 1945.

If your request is urgent you may call and charge your certificates to your visa or mastercard. There is a $10.00 fee for this service.

TENNESSEE DEPARTMENT OF HEALTH AND ENVIRONMENT
Vital Records
APPLICATION FOR CERTIFIED COPY OF CERTIFICATE OF BIRTH
Do Not Send Cash. Check Or Money Order Preferred.

DATE: _____

Full Name at Birth_____
           First   Middle   Last

Indicate Any Legal Changes of Names _____

Date of Birth _____ Sex _____
         Month   Day   Year

Place of Birth_____
        City   County   State

Full Name of Father_____ Race _____

Full Maiden Name of Mother_____ Race _____

Last Name of Mother at Time of Birth _____

Name of Doctor or Attendant at Birth (if known)_____

Hospital Where Birth Occurred _____

Next Older Brother or Sister_____ Younger_____

Signature of Person Making Request_____

Relationship _____

Purpose of Copy _____

Telephone number where you may be reached for additional information _____

All items must be completed in order for us to process your request.

Indicate number of each type of Certificate desired and enclose appropriate fee.

For years 1950—Current

☐   —Short Form (a certified transcript that shows Child's Name, Birth Date, Sex, County of Birth, Certificate Number and File Date)

☐   —Long Form (a certified copy showing all information)

Years prior to 1950

☐ Copies

The above fees are charged for the search of our records, and to include one copy, if record is on file in this office.

It is unlawful to willfully and knowingly make any false statement on this application.

PH-1654
VR Rev. 10/85

— —

DO NOT DETACH

This is a mailing insert. PRINT name and address of person
to whom the certified copy is to be mailed.

Name: _____

Street or
Route: _____

City or
Town: _____ State: _____ Zip: _____

PH-1654
VR Rev. 10/85

APPLICATION FOR A CERTIFIED COPY OF A CERTIFICATE OF MARRIAGE

Date _____

Number of
Copies Requested _____

Name of Groom _____
　　　　　　　　　　First　　　　　　　　　Middle　　　　　　　　　Last

Name of Bride at Birth _____
　　　　　　　　　　　First　　　　　　　　Middle　　　　　　　　　Last

Place This License Was Issued _____
　　　　　　　　　　　　　　County　　　　　　　　　　　　State

Date of Marriage _____
　　　　　　　　Month　　　　　　　　　Day　　　　　　　　　Year

Place of Marriage _____
　　　　　　　　City　　　　　　　　County　　　　　　　　State

Signature of Person Making Request _____

Relationship of Requester _____

Purpose of Copy _____

DO NOT DETACH

IMPORTANT

ENCLOSE FEE OF　　　　　　　FOR EACH COPY REQUESTED
Make check or money order payable to the TENNESSEE DEPARTMENT OF PUBLIC HEALTH
Fee Will Be Charged For Search And Cannot Be Refunded

This is a mailing insert. PRINT name and address of
person to whom the certified copy is to be mailed.

_____

Name _____
Street or
Route _____
City or
Town _____ Zip _____

PH-1670
VR Rev. 8/82

TENNESSEE DEPARTMENT OF HEALTH & ENVIRONMENT
Vital Records

APPLICATION FOR CERTIFIED COPY OF CERTIFICATE OF DEATH
Remit fee of   for each copy requested
Make check or money order payable to the TENNESSEE DEPARTMENT OF HEALTH & ENVIRONMENT
Do Not Send Cash. Check or Money Order Preferred.

DATE _____   Number of Copies Requested: _____

Name of Deceased _____
　　　　　　　　　first　　　　　　　　　middle　　　　　　　　　last

Date of Death _____
　　　　　　　month　　　　　　　　day　　　　　　　　year

Sex _____ Race _____ Age _____

Place of Death_____
　　　　　　city　　　　　　　　county　　　　　　　　state

Name of Funeral Home _____

Location of Funeral Home _____
　　　　　　　　city　　　　　　　state

Signature of Person Making Request: _____

Relationship to Deceased: _____

Purpose of Copy: _____

Telephone Number Where You May Be Reached:_____

A fee of   is charged for the search of our records even if no record is found, and includes one copy if a record is on file in this office.

(It is unlawful to willfully and knowingly make any false statement on this application.)   PH-1663
VR Rev. 5/85

DO NOT DETACH

Mail Copy To:

This is a mailing insert. PRINT name and address of person to whom the certified copy is to be mailed.

_____

_NAME_____
Street or
Route _____
City or
Town _____ State _____ Zip _____

PH-1663
VR Rev. 5/85

TEXAS

Send your requests to:

Texas State Department of Health
Bureau of Vital Statistics
1100 West 49th Street
Austin, Texas 78756-3191

(512) 458-7111

Send your requests for Marriage Certificates to:

County Clerk
County Court House
(County where the Marriage License was issued)

Cost for a certified Birth Certificate	$7.50
Cost for a wallet size Birth Certificate	$5.00
Cost for a certified Death Certificate	$7.50
Cost for a duplicate copy, when ordered at the same time	$2.00

The Texas State Department of Health has birth and death records from January 1, 1903.

TEXAS DEPARTMENT OF HEALTH
BUREAU OF VITAL STATISTICS
1100 WEST 49th STREET
AUSTIN, TEXAS 78756-3191

APPLICATION FOR CERTIFICATION OF BIRTH

WARNING — The penalty for knowingly making a false statement in this form can be 2-10 years in prison and a fine of up to $5,000. (Article 4477c, Revised Civil Statutes of Texas)

INSTRUCTIONS

THE FEE FOR EACH CERTIFICATION MUST BE SUBMITTED WITH THIS APPLICATION.

REMITTANCES MUST BE MADE PAYABLE TO THE TEXAS DEPARTMENT OF HEALTH.

MAIL THIS APPLICATION TO
BUREAU OF VITAL STATISTICS
Texas Department of Health
1100 West 49th St.
Austin, Texas 78756-3191

COPIES REQUESTED

CERTIFICATION OF BIRTH — HOW MANY [ ]

CERTIFICATION OF BIRTH (POCKETBOOK SIZE)** — HOW MANY [ ]

AMOUNT OF MONEY ENCLOSED

DO NOT WRITE IN THIS SPACE

REQUEST NO. AND DATE

AMOUNT

CODE

INFORMATION ABOUT PERSON WHOSE BIRTH CERTIFICATE IS REQUESTED (TYPE OR PRINT)

1. FULL NAME OF PERSON	FIRST NAME	MIDDLE NAME	LAST NAME
2. DATE OF BIRTH	MONTH	DAY / YEAR	3. SEX
4. PLACE OF BIRTH	CITY OR TOWN	COUNTY	STATE
5. FULL NAME OF FATHER	FIRST NAME	MIDDLE NAME	LAST NAME
6. FULL MAIDEN NAME OF MOTHER	FIRST NAME	MIDDLE NAME	LAST NAME

PERSON REQUESTING CERTIFICATION OF BIRTH

7. DO YOU WANT THE NAMES OF THE PARENTS SHOWN ON THE CERTIFICATION OF BIRTH?   YES [ ]   NO [ ]

8. PURPOSE FOR WHICH CERTIFICATION OF BIRTH IS TO BE USED (School, Employment, Military Service, Passport, Etc.)

9. RELATIONSHIP TO PERSON NAMED IN ITEM 1 ABOVE (Self, Mother, Attorney, Employer, Etc.)

10. SIGNATURE OF APPLICANT

11. DATE SIGNED

12. ADDRESS OF APPLICANT (Type or Print) — STREET ADDRESS — CITY OR TOWN — STATE — ZIP CODE

IF YOU WANT THE CERTIFICATION OF BIRTH MAILED TO SOME OTHER PERSON, COMPLETE THIS SECTION

TYPE OR PRINT — NAME — STREET ADDRESS — CITY OR TOWN — STATE — ZIP CODE

VS-141, REV. 1/82

*THE FEE FOR EACH CERTIFICATION OF BIRTH IS   REGARDLESS OF SIZE.

**A CERTIFICATION OF BIRTH (POCKETBOOK SIZE) INCLUDES ONLY THE INFORMATION SHOWN IN THE SAMPLE AT RIGHT.

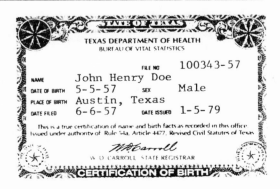

STATE OF TEXAS
TEXAS DEPARTMENT OF HEALTH
BUREAU OF VITAL STATISTICS
FILE NO 100343-57
NAME John Henry Doe
DATE OF BIRTH 5-5-57 SEX Male
PLACE OF BIRTH Austin, Texas
DATE FILED 6-6-57 DATE ISSUED 1-5-79
This is a true certification of name and birth facts as recorded in this office. Issued under authority of Rule 54a, Article 4477, Revised Civil Statutes of Texas
W. D. CARROLL STATE REGISTRAR
CERTIFICATION OF BIRTH

ACTUAL SIZE 2½" X 3¾"

TEXAS DEPARTMENT OF HEALTH
BUREAU OF VITAL STATISTICS
1100 WEST 49TH STREET
AUSTIN, TEXAS 78756

APPLICATION FOR CERTIFIED COPY OF DEATH CERTIFICATE

I N S T R U C T I O N S

The fee for a certified copy of a death certificate is   If more than one
certification of the same record is requested at the same time, the fee for the
first copy is   and the fee for each additional copy is

1. NAME _____ 2. SEX _____
            Given Name(s)   Last Name at Time of Death

3. DATE OF DEATH _____
            Month   Day   Year
      If unknown, show year last known to have been alive _____

4. PLACE OF DEATH _____
            City or Town   County
      If unknown, show last known county of residence _____

5. NAME OF FATHER _____

6. NAME OF MOTHER _____

7. I AM RELATED TO THE DECEASED AS _____

8. MY PURPOSE IN OBTAINING THE COPY IS _____

9. ENCLOSED IS A FEE OF $ _____ FOR _____ CERTIFIED COPY OR COPIES.

_____
SIGNATURE OF APPLICANT

_____
STREET ADDRESS

_____   _____
DATE OF APPLICATION   CITY AND STATE

VS-141.1
Rev. 1/82

UTAH

Send your requests to:

Bureau of Health Statistics
Utah State Department of Health
288 North 1460 West
P.O. Box 16700
Salt Lake City, Utah 84116-0700

(801) 538-6380

Send your requests for Marriage Certificates to:

County Clerk
County Court House
(County where the Marriage License was issued)

Cost for a certified Birth Certificate	$10.00
Cost for a certified Death Certificate	$ 7.00
Cost for a duplicate copy, when ordered at the same time	$ 3.00

The Utah Bureau of Health Statistics has birth and death records from January 1, 1905.

APPLICATION FOR CERTIFIED COPY OF A BIRTH CERTIFICATE

INFORMATION

Certificates for births that occurred in Utah since 1905 are on file in this office. Persons who were born in Utah and have no birth certificate on file may make application to file a Delayed Registration of Birth. Application forms for Delayed Registration of Birth must be obtained from this office. It is a violation of Utah State law for any person to obtain, possess, use, sell or furnish for any purpose of deception, a birth certificate or certified copy thereof.

INSTRUCTIONS—FEES ARE EFFECTIVE JULY 25, 1981

1. An application must be completed for each birth certificate requested.

2. If the applicant is not the person whose birth certificate is being requested, the reason for requesting the record must be provided.

3. There is a fee of _____ for each search of our files. The search includes the year the event is reported to have occurred and two years on either side of that year. Each additional five years to be searched requires an additional fee of _____ The entire file of birth certificates from 1905 to the present will be searched for the fee of _____ One certified copy of the record is issued, or a certificate of search if the record is not found. Additional certified copies of this record ordered at the same time are _____ each.

4. Send the completed application and required fee to the Bureau of Health Statistics, 288 North 1460 West, P.O. Box 16700, Salt Lake City, Utah 84116-0700.

IDENTIFYING INFORMATION

FULL NAME OF CHILD AT BIRTH _____

DATE OF BIRTH _____

PLACE OF BIRTH (City) _____ (County) _____

FULL NAME OF FATHER _____

BIRTHPLACE OF FATHER _____

FULL MAIDEN NAME OF MOTHER _____

BIRTHPLACE OF MOTHER _____

APPLICANT

Reason for Requesting Certified Copy (include your relationship to the person whose certificate is being requested).

_____

Signature of Applicant _____ Date _____

Address of Applicant _____

_____ Telephone Number _____

Number of copies requested _____ Amount of Fee $ _____

If copies are to be mailed to address other than above, specify name and mailing address _____

_____

APPLICATION FOR CERTIFIED COPY OF A DEATH CERTIFICATE

INFORMATION

**Death certificates for deaths that occurred in
Utah since 1905 are on file in this office.**

INSTRUCTIONS—FEES ARE EFFECTIVE JULY 25, 1981

1. An application must be completed for each death certificate requested.

2. If the applicant is not a member of the immediate family of the deceased person, the reason for requesting the record must be provided.

3. There is a fee of _____ for each search of our files. The search includes the year the event is reported to have occurred and two years on either side of that year. Each additional five years to be searched requires an additional fee of _____ The entire file of death certificates from 1905 to the present will be searched for the fee of _____ . One certified copy of the record is issued, or a certificate of search if the record is not found. Additional certified copies of the same record ordered at the same time are _____ each.

4. Send the completed application and required fee to the Bureau of Health Statistics, 288 North 1460 West, P.O. Box 16700, Salt Lake City, Utah 84116-0700.

IDENTIFYING INFORMATION

FULL NAME OF DECEASED _____

Date of Death _____ (If not known, give date last known alive) _____

Place of Death (City) _____ (County) _____

Birthplace of Decedent (State or Country) _____ Date of Birth of Decedent _____

Usual Residence of Decedent (City & State) _____

Full Name of Father _____

Full Maiden Name of Mother _____

If Deceased was Married, Name of Spouse _____

APPLICANT

Reason for Requesting Certified Copy (include your relationship to the person whose certificate is being requested).

_____

Signature of Applicant _____ Date _____

Address of Applicant _____

_____ Telephone Number _____

Number of copies requested _____ Amount of Fee $ _____

If copies are to be mailed to address other than above, specify name and mailing address

_____
        Name   *Address*

VERMONT

Send your requests to:

Vermont Department of Health
Public Health Statistics
P.O. Box 70
Burlington, Vermont 05402

(802) 863-7275

Send your requests for records from 1760 to 1954 to:

Vermont Public Records Division
State Administration Building
Montpelier, Vermont 05602

(802) 863-7300

Cost for a certified Birth Certificate	$5.00
Cost for a short form Birth Certificate	$2.00
Cost for a certified Marriage Certificate	$5.00
Cost for a certified Death Certificate	$5.00

The Vermont Public Records Division has records from 1760 to 1954. For records from January 1, 1954 write to the Vermont Department of Health.

Circle the year-group(s) you
  wish to have searched:

1760-1870

      1870-1908

1909-1941

      1942-1954

STATE OF VERMONT

BIRTH APPLICATION

This document is needed for:
  (Please check)

Passport_____

Retirement_____

Legal Matter_____

Genealogy_____

Other (Specify)_____

INSTRUCTIONS

1. Please print or type all information clearly.
2. Enclose check or money order (no cash, please) in amount of _____ to cover cost of search of our files and one certified copy, if record is found. Name and address on check, please!
3. Make sure check or money order is made payable only to "Public Records Division".
   Mail completed application form and fee to: Public Records Division, State Administration Building, Montpelier, VT 05602.
4. Enclose stamped. self-addressed envelope.
5. If person named on line 1 below is not yourself, please indicate his/her relationship to you:

_____

1. NAME AT BIRTH_____
                  (First)   (Middle)   (Last)

2. DATE OF BIRTH_____SEX_____
               (Mo)   (Day)   (Year)

3. PLACE OF BIRTH_____
                 (Town/City)   (County)

4. FATHER_____BIRTHPLACE_____

5. MOTHER_____BIRTHPLACE_____

6. NO. OF CHILD OF MOTHER__(1st, 2nd, 3rd, etc.)_____

OFFICE USE ONLY
Fee enclosed Yes___No___
Record found Yes___No___
Record sent Yes___No___
Year-group searched:
1760-1870   1870-1908
1909-1941   1942-1954
Searched by_____
_____
_____

APPLICANT INFORMATION

       Mr.
Name Mrs. _____
       Miss
Street/RFD_____

City/Town_____

State_____Zip_____

Signature_____

           Date_____

Circle the year-group(s) you
wish to have searched:

1760-1870

        1870-1908

1909-1941

        1942-1954

STATE OF VERMONT

MARRIAGE APPLICATION

This document is needed for
(Please check)

Passport_____

Retirement_____

Legal Matter_____

Genealogy_____

Other (Specify)_____

INSTRUCTIONS

1. Please print or type all information clearly.
2. Enclose check or money order (no cash, please) in amount of _____ to cover cost of search of our files and one certified copy, if record is found. Name and address on check, please.
3. Make sure check or money order is made payable only to "Public Records Division".
Mail completed application form and fee to: Public Records Division, State Administration Building, Montpelier, VT 05602.
4. Enclose stamped, self-addressed envelope.
5. If neither party named in marriage below is yourself, please indicate relationship to you:

_____

DATE OF MARRIAGE_____   PLACE OF MARRIAGE_____

GROOM: BRIDE :

_____   _____

FATHER_____   FATHER_____

MOTHER_____   MOTHER_____

AGE OF GROOM_____   AGE OF BRIDE_____

BIRTHPLACE_____   BIRTHPLACE_____

OTHER INFORMATION_____   OTHER INFORMATION_____

_____   _____

OFFICE USE ONLY

Fee enclosed Yes____ No____
Record found Yes____ No____
Record sent Yes____ No____
Year-group searched:
    1760-1870   1870-1908
    1909-1941   1942-1954

Searched by_____

_____
_____

APPLICANT INFORMATION

       Mr.
Name Mrs._____
       Miss
Street/RFD_____

City/Town_____

State_____Zip_____

Signature_____

                Date_____

Circle the year-group(s) you
wish to have searched:

1760-1870

      1870-1908

1909-1941

      1942-1954

STATE OF VERMONT

This document is needed for:
(Please check)

Legal Matter_____

Genealogy_____

Other (Specify)_____

DEATH APPLICATION

INSTRUCTIONS

1. Please print or type all information clearly.
2. Enclose check or money order (no cash, please) in amount of _____ to cover cost of search of our files and one certified copy, if record is found. Name and address on check, please.
3. Make sure check or money order is made payable to "Public Records Division".
   Mail completed application form and fee to: Public Records Division, State Administration Building, Montpelier, VT 05602.
4. Enclose stamped, self-addressed envelope.
5. Indicate relationship of person on line 1 below to yourself:_____

1. NAME AT DEATH_____
                    (First)   (Middle)   (Last)

2. DATE OF DEATH_____SEX_____
                 (Mo)   (Day)   (Year)

3. PLACE OF DEATH_____AGE_____

4. BIRTHPLACE_____SPOUSE_____

5. NAME OF FATHER_____

6. MAIDEN NAME OF MOTHER_____

7. OTHER HELPFUL INFORMATION_____

OFFICE USE ONLY		
Fee enclosed	Yes___	No___
Record found	Yes___	No___
Record sent	Yes___	No___
Year-group searched:		
1760-1870	1870-1908	
1909-1941	1942-1954	

Searched by_____
_____
_____

APPLICANT INFORMATION
_____
          Mr.
Name Mrs._____
          Miss
Street/RFD_____

City/Town_____

State_____Zip_____

Signature_____

                Date_____

VIRGINIA

Send your requests to:

Virginia Department of Health
Division of Vital Records
James Madison Building
P.O. Box 1000
Richmond, Virginia 23208-1000

(804) 786-6221

Cost for a certified Birth Certificate	$5.00
Cost for a certified Marriage Certificate	$5.00
Cost for a certified Death Certificate	$5.00

The Virginia Division of Vital Records has records from January 1, 1853. Birth and death records were not routinely filed between 1896 and 1912.

VS6—10/84

COMMONWEALTH OF VIRGINIA
APPLICATION FOR A CERTIFIED COPY OF A BIRTH RECORD

1 FULL NAME AT BIRTH		**DO NOT WRITE IN THIS SPACE**
2 DATE OF BIRTH	SEX ‖ COLOR OR RACE	
3 PLACE OF BIRTH	**VIRGINIA**	
4 FULL NAME OF FATHER	ENCLOSED IS $ _____	SEARCHED BY _____
5 FULL MAIDEN NAME OF MOTHER	FOR _____ CERTIFIED COPIES.	☐ INDEX ☐ DF ☐ BOOK ☐ HOS
6 NAME OF PHYSICIAN OR MIDWIFE AT BIRTH (IF KNOWN)	NOTE: IF SHORT FORM BIRTH CARD DESIRED, CHECK HERE ☐	RECHECKED BY _____
7 NAME OF HOSPITAL (IF ANY) WHERE BIRTH OCCURRED		
8 HAS ORIGINAL NAME EVER BEEN CHANGED OTHER THAN BY MARRIAGE? YES ☐ NO ☐ IF SO, WHAT WAS ORIGINAL NAME?		I.N.
9 ARE YOU THE PERSON NAMED IN LINE 1? YES ☐ NO ☐ IF NOT, WHAT IS YOUR RELATIONSHIP?		
10 SPECIFIC PURPOSE FOR WHICH THIS CERTIFIED COPY IS REQUESTED		
11 SIGNATURE OF APPLICANT ▶		
12 STREET ADDRESS		
13 CITY, STATE AND ZIP CODE		ISSUED

DO NOT REMOVE THIS STUB

IMPORTANT

Virginia statutes require a fee of _____ be charged for each certification of a vital record or for a search of the files when no certification is made. Make check or money order payable to STATE HEALTH DEPARTMENT.

Birth records were not routinely filed during period 1896-1912. If birth occurred then, or if no record is on file, other types of evidence may be acceptable to using agencies.

Birth records are, by statute, confidential. Certifications may be issued to the individual registrant, members of the registrant's immediate family, the registrant's guardian, their respective legal representative, or by court order.

Warning: Making a false application for a vital record is a prosecutable offense under state as well as federal law.

PLEASE NOTE!
PRINT YOUR NAME AND COMPLETE MAILING ADDRESS IN THIS SPACE—THIS IS A MAILING INSERT AND WILL BE USED TO MAIL THE CERTIFIED COPY TO YOU.
THANK YOU!

NAME
STREET OR ROUTE
CITY OR TOWN, STATE, ZIP CODE

Send to:
Division of Vital Records
P.O. Box 1000
Richmond, Virginia 23208-1000

COMMONWEALTH OF VIRGINIA
APPLICATION FOR A CERTIFIED COPY OF A MARRIAGE RECORD

		DO NOT WRITE IN THIS SPACE
1 FULL NAME OF HUSBAND		
2 FULL MAIDEN NAME OF WIFE		1st SEARCH BY ☐ INDEX ☐ BOOK
3 DATE OF MARRIAGE	COLOR OR RACE	2nd SEARCH BY ☐ INDEX ☐ BOOK
4 CITY OR COUNTY IN WHICH MARRIAGE LICENSE WAS ISSUED	VIRGINIA	CERTIFICATE NUMBER
5 SPECIFIC PURPOSE FOR WHICH THIS CERTIFIED COPY IS REQUESTED		
6 SIGNATURE OF APPLICANT ➤		
7 STREET ADDRESS		
8 CITY, STATE AND ZIP CODE		ISSUED

ENCLOSED IS $_____ FOR _____ CERTIFIED COPIES ($5.00 EACH)

DO NOT REMOVE THIS STUB

IMPORTANT

As required by statute, a fee of   is charged for each certification of a vital record or for a search of the files when no certification is made. Make check or money order payable to the STATE HEALTH DEPARTMENT. Give all information possible in above application for record. If exact date is unknown, give approximate year of marriage.

Certifications of marriage records may also be obtained from Clerk of Court in city or county in which marriage license was issued.

PLEASE NOTE!

PRINT YOUR NAME AND COMPLETE MAILING ADDRESS IN THIS SPACE—

THIS IS A MAILING INSERT AND WILL BE USED TO MAIL THE CERTIFIED COPY TO YOU.

THANK YOU!

Send To:

Bureau of Vital Records
P.O. Box 1000
Richmond, Virginia 23208-1000

NAME
STREET OR ROUTE
CITY OR TOWN, STATE, ZIP CODE

VS7—7/83

			DO NOT WRITE IN THIS SPACE
1 FULL NAME OF DECEASED			
2 DATE OF DEATH	SEX	COLOR OR RACE	
3 PLACE OF DEATH	VIRGINIA		
4 NAME OF HOSPITAL (IF ANY) WHERE DEATH OCCURRED			1st SEARCH BY _____ ☐ INDEX ☐ BOOK ☐ HOSP.
5 IF MARRIED, NAME OF HUSBAND OR WIFE			2nd SEARCH BY _____ ☐ INDEX ☐ BOOK ☐ HOSP.
6 NAME OF FUNERAL DIRECTOR (IF KNOWN)			CERTIFICATE NUMBER
7 ADDRESS OF FUNERAL DIRECTOR			
8 HOW ARE YOU RELATED TO THE PERSON NAMED ON LINE 1?			
9 SPECIFIC PURPOSE FOR WHICH THIS CERTIFIED COPY IS REQUESTED			
10 SIGNATURE OF APPLICANT ➤			
11 STREET ADDRESS			
12 CITY, STATE AND ZIP CODE			
ENCLOSED IS $_____ FOR_____ CERTIFIED COPIES			ISSUED

DO NOT REMOVE THIS STUB

IMPORTANT

Virginia statutes require a fee of _____ for a certification of a death record or for a search of the files when no certification is issued. Make check or money order payable to STATE HEALTH DEPARTMENT.

Death records were not routinely filed during period 1896-1912. However, some records are available in the health departments of a few of the larger cities.

Death records are, by statute, confidential. Certifications may be issued to surviving relatives, their legal representatives, an authorized agency acting in their behalf, or by court order.

Warning: Making a false application for a vital record is a prosecutable offense under state as well as federal law.

NAME
STREET OR ROUTE
CITY OR TOWN, STATE, ZIP CODE

PLEASE NOTE!

PRINT YOUR NAME AND COMPLETE MAILING ADDRESS IN THIS SPACE— THIS IS A MAILING INSERT.

THANK YOU!

Send To:
Bureau of Vital Records
P.O. Box 1000
Richmond, Virginia 23208-1000

WASHINGTON

Send your requests to:

Washington State Department
of Social and Health Services
Vital Records
P.O. Box 9709, ET-11
Olympia, Washington 98504

(206) 753-5936

Cost for a certified Birth Certificate	$11.00
Cost for a certified Marriage Certificate	$11.00
Cost for a certified Death Certificate	$11.00

The Washington Office of Vital Records has birth and death records from July 1, 1907 and marriage records from January 1, 1968. If no record is found $3.00 of the fee will be returned to you.

VITAL RECORDS
P.O. Box 9709, ET-11
Olympia, WA 98504

Please specify type of Record desired ("X")

	Birth		Marriage
	Death		Divorce

_____ FULL CERTIFIED COPIES (Birth, Marriage / Death, Divorce) Suitable for any purpose

_____ BIRTH CARDS Not accepted for passports or by some agencies

FOR OFFICE USE ONLY

1. Name on Record _____
   Last   First   Middle

2. Spouse of Line 1 _____
   Marriage/Divorce Only

3. Date of Event _____
   Month   Day   Year

4. Place of Event _____ **Washington**
   City   County

5. Father's Name _____
   Last   First   Middle

6. Mother's Birth Name _____
   Last   First   Middle

7. Your Relationship to Line 1 _____

8. Your Phone Number _____

PRESS HARD

Name _____

Street Address _____

City _____ State _____ Zip _____

SEE REVERSE FOR ADDITIONAL INFORMATION

YOUR MAILING ADDRESS

For Birth Only
If an adopted child, put X in this square ☐
If a delayed filing, put X in this square ☐

FOR OFFICE USE ONLY

Certificate No. _____
Index (Fiche) _____
Index (Computer) _____
Delayed Index _____
NR Letter _____
More Info Letter _____

Date Photo Copy _____

Cards _____

Affidavit _____

Paternity/Consent _____

By _____

Refund $ _____

Check No. _____

THIS FORM REPLACES ALL PREVIOUS APPLICATIONS

DSHS 9-622 (REV. 9-83)

WEST VIRGINIA

Send your requests to:

West Virginia State Health Department
Division of Vital Statistics
Charleston, West Virginia 25305

(304) 348-2931

Cost for a certified Birth Certificate	$5.00
Cost for a certified Marriage Certificate	$5.00
Cost for a certified Death Certificate	$5.00

The West Virginia Division of Vital Statistics has birth and death records from January 1, 1917 and marriage records from January 1, 1964. Make check payable to "Division of Vital Statistics." The Division does not have a separate form for requesting a copy of a marriage certificate. For records prior to 1964 write to the county clerk in the county where the marriage took place.

If your request is urgent you may call and charge your certificates to your visa or mastercard. There is a $5.00 fee for this service.

APPLICATION FOR CERTIFIED COPY OF CERTIFICATE OF BIRTH OR DEATH

WEST VIRGINIA DEPARTMENT OF HEALTH — DIVISION OF VITAL STATISTICS

CHARLESTON, WEST VIRGINIA 25305

FOR OFFICE USE ONLY

WHEN STAMPED PAID THIS IS YOUR RECEIPT	
CASH	
CHECK	
MONEY ORD.	
NO. COPIES	
AMOUNT	

NOTE: FEE OF _____ FOR EACH COPY MUST ACCOMPANY THIS APPLICATION CASH IS SENT AT SENDERS RISK. PLEASE SEND ME_____COPIES.

BIRTH CERTIF. ◄ **CHECK ONE** ► DEATH CERTIF.

HAVE COUNTY RECORDS BEEN SEARCHED? YES ☐ NO ☐

BIRTH OR DEATH

NAME— FIRST　　　MIDDLE　　　LAST

DATE— MONTH　　　DAY　　　YEAR

PLACE— CITY OR POST OFFICE　　　COUNTY　　　STATE

ONLY BIRTH

FATHER'S NAME— FIRST　　　MIDDLE　　　LAST

MAIDEN NAME OF MOTHER— FIRST　　　MIDDLE　　　LAST

ONLY DEATH

NAME OF FUNERAL DIRECTOR—

◁ PLEASE PRINT NAME AND ADDRESS OF PERSON TO WHOM CERTIFICATE IS TO BE MAILED.

WHAT IS YOUR RELATIONSHIP TO THE PERSON NAMED ON THE CERTIFICATE?

PLEASE PRINT - DO NOT WRITE

WISCONSIN

Send your requests to:

Wisconsin Department of Health and Social Services
Section of Vital Statistics
1 West Wilson Street
P.O. Box 309
Madison, Wisconsin 53701-0309

(608) 266-0330

Cost for a certified Birth Certificate	$8.00
Cost for a certified Marriage Certificate	$5.00
Cost for a certified Death Certificate	$5.00
Cost for a duplicate copy, when ordered at the same time	$2.00

The Wisconsin Department of Health has records as early as 1814, but prior to January 1, 1907 less than half of the records were ever filed. The Department has a list of the earliest records on file arranged by county.

If your request is urgent you may call and charge your certificates to your visa or mastercard. There is a $5.00 charge for this service.

SEARCHES

The following information is needed to enable us to conduct a <u>thorough</u> search of our files:

<u>BIRTH RECORD:</u>

Name at Birth: _____ _____

Date of Birth: _____

Parents Names: (include mother's maiden) _____

Place of Birth (<u>City, County:</u> _____

<u>DEATH RECORD:</u>

Name of Decedent: _____

Date of Death: _____

Place of Death: (City, County) _____

Age of Decedent: _____   Spouse Name: _____

Parents Names: _____   Decedent Occupation: _____

Decedent SS# _____

<u>MARRIAGE RECORD:</u>

Name of Groom: _____

Name of Bride: _____

Date of Marriage: _____

Place of Marriage: <u>(city, county especially important)</u> _____

FEE: The statutory searching fee is to be collected for a search of our files for
       each record requested. This <u>fee is not refundable</u> in the event that the record
       is not on file. If the requested record is located, one copy of the record
       will be sent without further charge.
       Please make your check or money order payable to:
       DEPARTMENT OF HEALTH & SOCIAL SERVICES

ADDRESS: Department of Health & Social Services
             Section of Vital Statistics
             P.O. Box 309
             Madison, WI 53701

RETURN ADDRESS: Name of Applicant: _____

                    Street Address: _____

                    City, State, Zip Code: _____

-- PLEASE INCLUDE A SELF-ADDRESSED STAMPED ENVELOPE --

WYOMING

Send your requests to:

Wyoming State Vital Records Services
Hathaway Building
Cheyenne, Wyoming 82002

(307) 777-7591

Cost for a certified Birth Certificate	$5.00
Cost for a certified Marriage Certificate	$5.00
Cost for a certified Death Certificate	$3.00

The Wyoming State Vital Records Services has birth and death records from July 1909 and marriage records from May 1941.

STATE OF WYOMING

APPLICATION FOR CERTIFIED COPY OF BIRTH CERTIFICATE

A request for a certified copy of a birth certificate should be submitted on this form along with the fee of _____ per copy. Money orders or checks should be made payable to VITAL RECORDS SERVICES. Please enclose a self-addressed, stamped envelope with this application.

Send to: Vital Records Services
                  Hathaway Building
                  Cheyenne, WY 82002

A searching fee of _____ per hour, or fraction thereof, is charged for any search which is made. If a record is found, you will receive either a certified copy or a verification with no additional charge.

If no record is found, instructions for filing a Delayed Birth Certificate will be sent if this application is signed by the registrant or a parent.

Amount Enclosed: $_____   Number of Copies: _____

Full Name at birth _____
                        First   Middle   Last

Date of Birth _____ Sex_____
                   Month   Day   Year

Place of Birth _____
                        City   County   State

Father's Name _____
                        First   Middle   Last

Mother's Maiden Name _____
                        First   Middle   Last

Signature of person whose certificate
is being requested or parent   _____

If under 19 years of age, signature of parent or legal guardian required. Legal guardian must submit a copy of guardianship papers.

If you are not named on the certificate, sign below indicating your relationship to the person whose certificate is being requested and stating the purpose for which it is needed.

_____

Address of Applicant _____

If copy(s) is (are) to be mailed to another person, give name and address and enclose a stamped envelope addressed to that person.

_____

VR 1-3

STATE OF WYOMING – DIVISION OF HEALTH AND MEDICAL SERVICES
Vital Records Services
Cheyenne, Wyoming 82002

APPLICATION FOR CERTIFIED COPY OF RECORD OF MARRIAGE OR DIVORCE

Certified copies bearing the state registered number, the seal and certification of the State Registrar are issued only by the Deputy State Registrar of Vital Records in Cheyenne.

For each certified copy of a record of marriage or divorce, a fee of   dollars must be paid by the person requesting the copy. Remittance must be made in advance in the form of money order, check or cash.

Type of record requested: Marriage _____   Divorce _____

Enclosed is $_____ for _____ certified copy(ies).

Name of Husband/Groom _____

Name of Wife/Bride _____

Date of Event _____

Place of Occurrence _____

If not named on certificate, purpose for which record is needed _____

_____

Signature of person making application _____

Your relationship to person whose certificate is requested _____

Address of Applicant _____

_____

If certified copy(ies) is to be mailed to another person, please give name and

address of that person _____

_____

VR 3-A

STATE OF WYOMING

APPLICATION FOR CERTIFIED COPY OF DEATH CERTIFICATE

A request for a certified copy of a death certificate should be submitted on this form along with the fee of _____ per copy. Money orders or checks should be made payable to VITAL RECORDS SERVICES. Please enclose a self-addressed, stamped envelope with this application.

Send to: Vital Records Services
                            Hathaway Building
                            Cheyenne, WY 82002

A searching fee of _____ per hour, or fraction thereof, is charged for any search which is made. If a record is found, you will receive either a certified copy or a verification with no additional charge.

Amount Enclosed: $_____ .   Number of Copies: _____

Full Name of Deceased _____
                         First   Middle   Last

Place of Death _____
                         City   County   State

Date of Death _____
                        Month   Day   Year

Surviving Spouse _____

SIGNATURE of person making application _____

Please indicate your relationship to the deceased and state the purpose for which the record is needed.

_____

Address of Applicant _____

If the copy(s) is (are) to be mailed to another person, give name and address and enclose a stamped envelope addressed to that person.

_____

VR 2-3

AMERICAN SAMOA

Send your requests to:

Registrar of Vital Statistics
Vital Statistics Section
LBJ Tropical Medical Center
Pago Pago, American Samoa 96799

(684) 633-1222

Cost for a certified Birth Certificate	$2.00
Cost for a certified Marriage Certificate	$2.00
Cost for a certified Death Certificate	$2.00

The Registrar has records from 1900. The Registrar, at this time, only issues an application form for birth certificates.

TO: _____

_____

_____

REFERENCE: _____

I REQUEST A CERTIFIED COPY OF MY BIRTH CERTIFICATE BE SENT TO THE
ABOVE ADDRESS TO ESTABLISH BIRTH IN THE UNITED STATES. THIS BIRTH
CERTIFICATE MUST HAVE A RAISED OR MULTI-COLORED STATE SEAL ON IT.
THE FOLLOWING INFORMATION IS PROVIDED TO ASSIST YOUR OFFICE IN
LOCATING MY BIRTH CERTIFICATE.

_____
SIGNATURE

NAME I WAS BORN UNDER:_____
FIRST   MIDDLE   MAIDEN   LAST

PLACE OF BIRTH:_____
CITY OR TOWN   COUNTY   STATE

DATE OF BIRTH:_____
MONTH   DAY   YEAR

SEX:_____ RACE:_____

FATHER'S NAME:_____
FIRST   MIDDLE   LAST

MOTHER'S MAIDEN NAME:_____
FIRST   MIDDLE   LAST

NAME OF HOSPITAL:_____

ENCLOSED FIND A MONEY ORDER IN THE AMMOUNT OF $_____

GUAM

Send your requests to:

Office of Vital Statistics
Department of Public Health and Social Services
P.O. Box 2816
Agana, Guam 96910

011 (671) 734-2951

Cost for a certified Birth Certificate	$2.00
Cost for a certified Marriage Certificate	$2.00
Cost for a certified Death Certificate	$2.00

The Office of Vital Statistics has birth, marriage, and death records from October 26, 1901.

OFFICE OF VITAL STATISTICS
Department of Public Health and Social Services
P.O. Box 2816
Agana, Guam 96910

APPLICATION FOR A COPY OF Birth ☐ Death ☐ Marriage ☐

<u>INFORMATION FOR APPLICANT</u>: It is absolutely essential that the name be accurately spelled and that the exact date - month, day and year - the exact place of birth, name of hospital be fully given in every application.

PRINT ALL ITEMS CLEARLY

1. NAME _____
      (First name)   (Middle)   (Last name at time of birth)

2. DATE OF BIRTH _____   DATE OF DEATH _____
      (Month)   (Day)   (Year)   DATE OF MARRIAGE _____

3. PLACE OF BIRTH _____   PLACE OF DEATH _____
      (Name of Hospital or village)

4. FATHER'S NAME _____
            (First)   (Middle)   (Last)

5. MOTHER'S MAIDEN NAME _____
                  (First)   (Middle)   (Last)

6. NUMBER OF COPIES DESIRED _____Certificate. NUMBER, IF KNOWN _____

7. _____
      Relationship to person named in Item one above. If self, state "SELF"

<u>NOTE:</u> Copy of a birth or death record can be issued only to persons to whom the record relates, if of age, or a parent or other lawful representative.

IF THIS REQUEST IS NOT FOR YOUR OWN BIRTH RECORD OR THAT OF YOUR CHILD, PROPER WRITTEN AUTHORIZATION FROM THE PERSON MUST BE PRESENTED WITH THIS APPLICATION.

SIGN YOUR NAME AND ADDRESS BELOW

NAME _____

ADDRESS _____

CITY _____ STATE _____ ZIP CODE _____

<u>FEE</u>

PURSUANT TO PUBLIC LAW 10-44, Section 9324, a fee of   is now being charged for each certified copy issued.

<u>APPLICANTS ARE ADVISED NOT TO SEND CASH BY MAIL.</u> Fees must be paid at time application is made.   Money order should be made payable to the Treasurer of Guam. Stamps and foreign currency cannot be accepted.

PANAMA CANAL ZONE

Send your requests to:

Vital Statistics Unit
Panama Canal Commission
APO Miami, 34011-5000

Cost for a certified Birth Certificate	$2.00
Cost for a certified Marriage Certificate	$2.00
Cost for a certified Death Certificate	$2.00

The Panama Canal Commission maintains and issues certificates for births, marriages, and deaths that occurred in the former Canal Zone from 1904 to September 30, 1979, when the Panama Canal Treaty became effective and the Canal Zone Government ceased to exist.

PANAMA CANAL COMMISSION

The Panama Canal Commission requires the payment of   for each copy issued of a birth, death or marriage certificate. Please complete this application and return it to the address below with the necessary amount. Money order should be made payable to the TREASURER, Panama Canal Commission, in U.S. currency.

This office maintains certificates ONLY for births, deaths or marriages that occurred in the former Canal Zone. For births, deaths or marriages that occurred in the Republic of Panama, write to: El Registro Civil, Apartado 5281, Panama 5, Republic of Panama.

....
(Date)

Vital Statistics Unit
Panama Canal Commission
Administrative Services Division
APO Miami   34011-5000

REGISTRAR:

Please issue................copy (copies) in ☐ English ☐ Spanish of the ☐ birth ☐ death ☐ marriage certificate requested below. I have attached $........................ (money order).

For Birth Certificate:

Name on Certificate ....

Date of Birth ....

Place of Birth...

Full Name of Father...

Mother's Maiden Name..

For Death Certificate:

Name of Deceased...

Date of Death ....

Place of Death..

For Marriage Certificate:

Name of parties: Male .... Female..

Date of Marriage .... Marriage License No. ....

Location of Marriage .... Balboa................................... Cristobal.

....
Signature of person applying for certificate

....
Relationship to person on certificate

Purpose desired ....

....
Mailing address (complete only if certificate is to be mailed).

PUERTO RICO

Send your requests to:

Puerto Rico Department of Health
Demographic Registry
P.O. Box 9342
San Juan, Puerto Rico 00908

(809) 728-7980

Cost for a certified Birth Certificate $2.00

Cost for a certified Marriage Certificate $2.00

Cost for a certified Death Certificate $2.00

The Puerto Rico Department of Health has vital records from June 22, 1931.

DEMOGRAPHIC REGISTRY AREA

BIRTH CERTIFICATE APPLICATION

Name at Birth: _____
            Father's last name   Mother's last name   Name

Date of Birth: _____
            Month   Day   Year

Place of Birth: _____
                                Town

Father's Name: _____

Mother's maiden Name: _____

Name of the Hospital: _____

Are you the person named in line #1? _____Yes _____No. If not,

what is your relationship with her or him _____

Specific purpose for which this certification is requested: _____

_____

Signature of Applicant: _____

Address where you want the certificate to be sent: _____

_____

Address of Applicant: _____

_____

Number of copies: _____.

Applicant IDENTIFICATION: _____Driving License _____Work

_____Passport _____Other   DATE: _____

IMPORTANT:

If event occurred from June 22, 1931 to present, you can apply with us to
the following address: Department of Health, Demographic Registry, P.O.
Box 9342, San Juan, Puerto Rico 00908.

If event occurred from 1885 to June 21, 1931 you must write to the municipality where the event occurred.

Please send a photocopy of an IDENTIFICATION with photography of applicant.

Applicant in Puerto Rico, please send a   Internal Revenue Stamp for
each copy requested.

Applicant out of Puerto Rico, please send a   money order for each
copy you need payable to"SECRETARY OF THE TREASURY" for each copy requested.

Please send us a pre-addressed envelope to mail your certificate.

_____
Direct Interest-Registrant, parents, their sons or legal representatives.

DEMOGRAPHIC REGISTRY AREA
MARRIAGE CERTIFICATE APPLICATION

Husband's Name: _____

Father's last name   Mother's last name   Name

Spouse's maiden Name: _____

Father's last name   Mother's last name   Name

Date of Marriage: _____

Month   Day   Year

Place of Marriage: _____

Town

Are you the person named in line #1? _____Yes _____No. If not,

what is your relationship with this person: _____.

Specific purpose for which this certification is requested: _____

_____.

Signature of Applicant: _____.

Applicant's address: _____

_____.

Address you want the certificate to be sent: _____

_____.

Number of copies: _____.

Applicant's IDENTIFICATION: _____Driving License _____Work

_____Passport _____Other DATE: _____

IMPORTANT:

If event occurred from June 22, 1931 to present you can apply with us to the following address: Department of Health, Demographic Registry, P.O. Box 9342, San Juan, Puerto Rico 00908.

If event occurred from 1885 to June 21, 1931 you must write to the municipality where the event occurred.

Please send a photocopy of an IDENTIFICATION with photography of applicant.

Applicant in Puerto Rico, please send Internal Revenue Stamp for each copy requested.

Applicant out of state, please send a money order payable to "SECRETARY OF THE TREASURY" for each copy requested.

Please send us a self addressed envelope to mail your certificate.

_____

Applicant's definition—contracting parties, parents, child or legal representative.

DEPARTMENT OF HEALTH
DEMOGRAPHIC REGISTRY AREA

DEATH CERTIFICATED APPLICATION

Deceased Name: _____

           Father's last name   Mother's last name   Name

Date of Death: _____

           Month   Day   Year

Place of Death: _____

           Town

Name of the Hospital: _____

Relationship with deceased: _____

Specific purpose for which this certification is requested: _____

_____

Applicant's signature: _____

Aplicant's address: _____

_____

Address where you want the certificate to be sent: _____

_____

Number of copies: _____

Applicant IDENTIFICATION: _____Driving License _____Work

_____Passport _____Other DATE: _____

IMPORTANT:

If event occurred from June 22, 1931 to present, you can apply with us to
the following address: Department of Health, Demographic Registry, P.O.
Box 9342, San Juan, Puerto Rico 00908.

If event occurred from 1885 to June 21, 1931 you must write to the municipality where the event occurred.

Please send a photocopy of an IDENTIFICATION with photography of applicant.

Applicant in Puerto Rico please send a   Internal Revenue Stamp for
each copy requested.

Applicant out of Puerto Rico send a   money order payable to "SE-
CRETARY OF THE TREASURY" for each copy requested.

Please send us a self addressed envelope to mail your certificate

_____

Applicant's definition-The funeral home, parents, child or legal representative of the deceased.

VIRGIN ISLANDS—
St. Croix

Send your requests to:

Virgin Islands Department of Health
Office of the Registrar of Vital Statistics
Charles Harwood Memorial Hospital
P.O. Box 520
Christiansted, St. Croix, Virgin Islands 00820

(809) 773-4050

Send your requests for Marriage Certificates to:

Chief Deputy Clerk
Territorial Court of the Virgin Islands
P.O. Box 929
St. Croix, Virgin Islands 00820

(809) 778-3350

Cost for a certified Birth Certificate	$5.00
Cost for a short form Birth Certificate	$3.00
Cost for a certified Death Certificate	$5.00

The Office has birth and death records from 1919.

VIRGIN ISLANDS OF THE UNITED STATES

DEPARTMENT OF HEALTH
OFFICE OF THE REGISTRAR OF VITAL STATISTICS

HD-ve   St. ———————————, Virgin Islands

APPLICATION FOR BIRTH RECORD

PLEASE PRINT OR TYPE: FAILURE TO COMPLETE THIS FORM PROPERLY MAY DELAY SERVICE TO YOU.

TYPE OF RECORD DESIRED (Check one)

VERIFICATION

A verification is a statement as to the date of birth and name of the child. A verification is used when it is necessary to prove age only.

CERTIFIED COPY

A certified copy is an abstract from the original birth certificate. It gives the name, sex, date and place of birth, certificate number, as well as the names of the parents.

An application for a certified copy of birth must be signed by the person named in the original certificate if 18 years or more or by a parent or legal representative of that person.

FEES: Send money order or check payable to the VIRGIN ISLANDS DEPARTMENT OF HEALTH.
(Please do not send cash)

FULL NAME	DATE OF BIRTH Or period to be searched.
PLACE OF BIRTH (City and Island)	
NAME FATHER	MAIDEN NAME MOTHER
AGE AT BIRTH	AGE AT BIRTH
BIRTHPLACE	BIRTHPLACE
ADDRESS (At time of birth)	ADDRESS (At time of birth)
PURPOSE FOR WHICH RECORD IS REQUIRED	SOCIAL SECURITY NUMBER

Your relationship to person whose record is required? If self, state "SELF"   _____

If attorney give name and relationship of your client to person whose record is required. _____

TO WHOM SHALL RECORD BE SENT?

Name_____

Address_____

City_____ State_____

Signature of Applicant_____

Address of Applicant_____

_____

Date _____

Sworn to and subscribed before me this _____ day of _____ 19_____ .

_____
(Signature and Seal of Notary Public)

VIRGIN ISLANDS OF THE UNITED STATES

DEPARTMENT OF HEALTH

OFFICE OF THE REGISTRAR OF VITAL STATISTICS

St. —————————————, Virgin Islands

HD-vf

•

APPLICATION FOR DEATH RECORD

PLEASE PRINT OR TYPE: FAILURE TO COMPLETE THIS FORM PROPERLY MAY DELAY SERVICE TO YOU.

TYPE OF RECORD DESIRED (Check one)

VERIFICATION	CERTIFIED COPY ☐ Fee
A verification is a statement as to the date of death and name of decedent. A verification is used as proof that the event occurred.	A certified copy is a replica of the original death certificate.
Anyone may apply for a verification of death.	Anyone who can establish that the record is needed for proof of parentage, social security and other benefits, settlement of estate, or for judicial or other proper purpose may apply for a certified copy.

FEES: Send money order or check payable to the VIRGIN ISLANDS DEPARTMENT OF HEALTH. **(PLEASE DO NOT SEND CASH)**

No fee is charged when the certificate is required by a local, state or federal government agency.

NAME OF DECEDENT	DATE OF DEATH OR PERIOD TO BE SEARCHED
PLACE OF DEATH (CITY AND ISLAND)	
NAME OF FATHER OF DECEDENT	MAIDEN NAME OF MOTHER OF DECEDENT
NUMBER OF COPIES DESIRED	CERTIFICATE NUMBER, IF KNOWN
PURPOSE FOR WHICH RECORD IS REQUIRED	

What is your relationship to decedent? _____

In what capacity are you acting? _____

If attorney, give name and relationship of your client to decedent. _____

TO WHOM SHALL RECORD BE SENT?	Signature of Applicant _____
Name _____	Address of Applicant _____
Address _____	_____
City _____ State _____	Date _____

VIRGIN ISLANDS—
St. Thomas and St. John

Send your requests to:

Virgin Islands Department of Health
Office of the Registrar of Vital Statistics
St. Thomas, Virgin Islands 00802

(809) 774-1734

Send your requests for Marriage Certificates to:

Court Clerk
Territorial Court of the Virgin Islands
P.O. Box 70
Charlotte Amalie, St. Thomas, Virgin Islands 00801

(809) 774-6680

Cost for a certified Birth Certificate	$5.00
Cost for a short form Birth Certificate	$3.00
Cost for a certified Marriage Certificate	$2.00
Cost for a certified Death Certificate	$5.00

The Office has birth records from July 1, 1906 and death records from January 1, 1906.

VIRGIN ISLANDS OF THE UNITED STATES

DEPARTMENT OF HEALTH

OFFICE OF THE REGISTRAR OF VITAL STATISTICS

HD-ve

St. ———————————————, Virgin Islands

APPLICATION FOR BIRTH RECORD

PLEASE PRINT OR TYPE: FAILURE TO COMPLETE THIS FORM PROPERLY MAY DELAY SERVICE TO YOU.

TYPE OF RECORD DESIRED (Check one)

VERIFICATION

A verification is a statement as to the date of birth and name of the child. A verification is used when it is necessary to prove age only.

CERTIFIED COPY

A certified copy is an abstract from the original birth certificate. It gives the name, sex, date and place of birth, certificate number, as well as the names of the parents.

An application for a certified copy of birth must be signed by the person named in the original certificate if 18 years or more or by a parent or legal representative of that person.

FEES: Send money order or check payable to the VIRGIN ISLANDS DEPARTMENT OF HEALTH.

(Please do not send cash)

FULL NAME	DATE OF BIRTH Or period to be searched.
PLACE OF BIRTH (City and Island)	
NAME FATHER	MAIDEN NAME MOTHER
AGE AT BIRTH	AGE AT BIRTH
BIRTHPLACE	BIRTHPLACE
ADDRESS (At time of birth)	ADDRESS (At time of birth)
PURPOSE FOR WHICH RECORD IS REQUIRED	SOCIAL SECURITY NUMBER

Your relationship to person whose record is required? If self, state "SELF". _____

If attorney give name and relationship of your client to person whose record is required. _____

TO WHOM SHALL RECORD BE SENT?

Name_____

Address_____

City_____State_____

Signature of Applicant_____

Address of Applicant_____

_____

Date _____

Sworn to and subscribed before me this _____ day of_____ 19_____.

_____
(Signature and Seal of Notary Public)

VIRGIN ISLANDS OF THE UNITED STATES

DEPARTMENT OF HEALTH
OFFICE OF THE REGISTRAR OF VITAL STATISTICS

St. – – – – – – – – – – – – – – –, Virgin Islands

HD-vf

●

APPLICATION FOR DEATH RECORD

PLEASE PRINT OR TYPE: FAILURE TO COMPLETE THIS FORM PROPERLY MAY DELAY SERVICE TO YOU.

TYPE OF RECORD DESIRED (Check one)

VERIFICATION	CERTIFIED COPY □ Fee
A verification is a statement as to the date of death and name of decedent. A verification is used as proof that the event occurred.	A certified copy is a replica of the original death certificate.
Anyone may apply for a verification of death.	Anyone who can establish that the record is needed for proof of parentage, social security and other benefits, settlement of estate, or for judicial or other proper purpose may apply for a certified copy.

FEES: Send money order or check payable to the VIRGIN ISLANDS DEPARTMENT OF HEALTH.
(PLEASE DO NOT SEND CASH)
No fee is charged when the certificate is required by a local, state or federal government agency.

NAME OF DECEDENT	DATE OF DEATH OR PERIOD TO BE SEARCHED
PLACE OF DEATH (CITY AND ISLAND)	
NAME OF FATHER OF DECEDENT	MAIDEN NAME OF MOTHER OF DECEDENT
NUMBER OF COPIES DESIRED	CERTIFICATE NUMBER, IF KNOWN
PURPOSE FOR WHICH RECORD IS REQUIRED	

What is your relationship to decedent? _____

In what capacity are you acting? _____

If attorney, give name and relationship of your client to decedent. _____

TO WHOM SHALL RECORD BE SENT?	Signature of Applicant _____
Name_____	Address of Applicant _____
Address_____	_____
City_____State_____	Date _____

CANADA—
Alberta

Send your requests to:

Social Services and Community Health
Division of Vital Statistics
Texaco Building
10130 112 Street
Edmonton, Alberta, Canada T5K 2P2

(403) 427-2683

Cost for a certified Birth Certificate	Can $7.00
Cost for a certified Marriage Certificate	Can $7.00
Cost for a certified Death Certificate	Can $7.00

The Alberta Division of Vital Statistics has birth records from 1853, marriage records from 1898, and death records from 1893. Make check payable to "Provincial Treasurer."

COUNTER

VITAL STATISTICS
APPLICATION FOR
CERTIFICATE OR SEARCH

SOCIAL SERVICES AND COMMUNITY HEALTH
DIVISION OF VITAL STATISTICS
TEXACO BUILDING, 10130 - 112 STREET
EDMONTON, ALBERTA T5K 2P2
PHONE: 427-2683

CERTIFICATES ARE   **EACH PAYABLE TO: PROVINCIAL TREASURER. Indicate quantity and size.**

IF BIRTH CERTIFICATE(S) REQUIRED COMPLETE THIS SECTION (please print)

			Quantity	Size
Surname (if married woman maiden surname)	(Given Names)	Sex ☐ M ☐ F	. . . .	☐ Wallet
Date of Birth: Month by Name / Day / Year	Place of Birth (city, town, or village): ALBERTA / Name of Hospital Where Birth Occurred:		. . . .	☐ Framing
			* RESTRICTED COPY	
Surname of Father: (Given Names)	Birth Place of Father:		. . . .	☐ certified copy * see note 4A
Maiden Surname of Mother: (Given Names)	Birth Place of Mother:		. . . .	☐ genealogical * see note 4B
Date of Registration:	Place of Registration:	Amendment Number:	Registration Number:	Searched/Verified:

IF MARRIAGE CERTIFICATE(S) REQUIRED COMPLETE THIS SECTION (please print)

			Quantity	Size
Surname of Groom: (Given Names)	Birth Place of Groom:		. . . .	☐ Wallet
			. . . .	☐ Framing
Maiden Surname of Bride: (Given Names)	Birth Place of Bride:		* RESTRICTED COPY	
				☐ certified copy * see note 4A
Date of Marriage: Month by Name / Day / Year	Place of Marriage (city, town, or village): ALBERTA		. . . .	☐ genealogical * see note 4B
Date of Registration:	Place of Registration:	Amendment Number:	Registration Number:	Searched/Verified:

IF DEATH CERTIFICATE(S) REQUIRED COMPLETE THIS SECTION (please print)

ONE SIZE ONLY

				Quantity	Size
Surname of Deceased:	(Given Names)	Age:	Sex: ☐ M ☐ F	. . . .	☐ Framing
Date of Death: Month by Name / Day / Year	Place of Death (city, town, or village): ALBERTA			* RESTRICTED COPY	
Usual Residence of Deceased Prior to Death:		Marital Status:		. . . .	☐ certified copy * see note 4A
				. . . .	☐ genealogical * see note 4B
Date of Registration:	Place of Registration:	Amendment Number:	Registration Number:	Searched/Verified:

I require these certificates for the following purpose:

. . . .

. . . .

State your Relationship to person named on certificate:

Signature of Applicant:
x

Your Reference No. (if applicable):

FOR OFFICE USE ONLY

CASH/CHEQUE

Amount $ . . . .

Mail Clerk: . . . .

Cashier: . . . .

Telephone Number:

Fee Enclosed
$

☐ N.I.Y.
☐ P/U
☐ C

PRINT CLEARLY, THIS IS YOUR MAILING ADDRESS

Name:

Street Address: Apt. No.:

City: Province: Postal Code:

Remarks:

P.L.U. Number:

SSCH-1050 (85/05)
DVS - 32 (85/05)

CANADA—
British Columbia

Send your requests to:

Province of British Columbia
Ministry of Health
Division of Vital Statistics
1515 Blanshard Street
Victoria, British Columbia, Canada V8W 3C8

(604) 387-0041

Cost for a certified Birth Certificate	Can $10.00
Cost for a certified Marriage Certificate	Can $10.00
Cost for a certified Death Certificate	Can $10.00

The British Columbia Ministry of Health has vital records from 1872 and some baptismal registers from 1849.

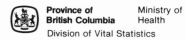

Province of British Columbia
Division of Vital Statistics

Ministry of Health

APPLICATION FOR SERVICE

YOUR FILE _____

MAILING ADDRESS:
PLEASE **PRINT** YOUR NAME AND ADDRESS
CLEARLY INCLUDING POSTAL CODE

NAME _____

ADDRESS _____

CITY & PROV. _____

POSTAL CODE _____

IF COMPANY,
ATTENTION _____

TELEPHONE No. _____ TODAY'S DATE _____ 19 ____

SHADED AREA FOR OFFICE USE ONLY

REFUND $ _____

PLEASE INDICATE TYPE AND NUMBER
OF CERTIFICATE(S) REQUIRED ————→

IF BIRTH CERTIFICATE(S) REQUIRED COMPLETE THIS SECTION   (PLEASE PRINT)

SURNAME (IF MARRIED WOMAN MAIDEN SURNAME)	(GIVEN NAMES)	SEX

SMALL
9.5 cm x 6.4 cm

MONTH BY NAME	DAY	YEAR	PLACE OF BIRTH (CITY, TOWN OR VILLAGE)

BRITISH COLUMBIA

SURNAME OF FATHER	(GIVEN NAMES)	BIRTHPLACE OF FATHER

MAIDEN SURNAME OF MOTHER	(GIVEN NAMES)	BIRTHPLACE OF MOTHER

LARGE
21.6 cm x 17.8 cm

REGISTRATION NUMBER	REGISTRATION DATE	AMENDMENT NO.

SEARCHED _____ VERIFIED _____

IF MARRIAGE CERTIFICATE(S) REQUIRED COMPLETE THIS SECTION   (PLEASE PRINT)

SURNAME OF GROOM	(GIVEN NAMES)	BIRTHPLACE OF GROOM

SMALL
9.5 cm x 6.4 cm

SURNAME OF BRIDE PRIOR TO MARRIAGE	(GIVEN NAMES)	BIRTHPLACE OF BRIDE

LARGE
21.6 cm x 17.8 cm

MONTH BY NAME	DAY	YEAR	PLACE OF MARRIAGE (CITY, TOWN OR VILLAGE)

BRITISH COLUMBIA

CERTIFIED PHOTOCOPY SEE NOTE 3

REGISTRATION NUMBER	REGISTRATION DATE	AMENDMENT NO.

SEARCHED _____ VERIFIED _____

IF DEATH CERTIFICATE(S) REQUIRED COMPLETE THIS SECTION   (PLEASE PRINT)

SURNAME OF DECEASED	(GIVEN NAMES)	AGE	SEX

MONTH	DATE OF DEATH DAY	YEAR	PLACE OF DEATH (CITY, TOWN OR VILLAGE)

BRITISH COLUMBIA

LARGE
21.6 cm x 17.8 cm

PERMANENT RESIDENCE OF DECEASED PRIOR TO DEATH	PLACE OF BIRTH

REGISTRATION NUMBER	REGISTRATION DATE	AMENDMENT NO.

SEARCHED _____ VERIFIED _____

STATE **YOUR** RELATIONSHIP TO THE PERSON NAMED IN APPLICATION

STATE **SPECIFIC REASON** WHY CERTIFICATION IS REQUIRED

FEE ENCLOSED

X _____
(WRITTEN SIGNATURE OF APPLICANT) (DO NOT PRINT)

$ _____

HLTH 430 86/01

ISLAND BUSINESS FORMS LTD.

62493

CANADA—
Manitoba

Send your requests to:

Manitoba Community Services
Vital Statistics
Norquay Building, Room 104
401 York Avenue
Winnipeg, Manitoba, Canada R3C OP8

(204) 945-3701

Cost for a certified Birth Certificate	Can $15.00
Cost for a certified Marriage Certificate	Can $15.00
Cost for a certified Death Certificate	Can $15.00

The Manitoba Office of Vital Statistics has records from 1882.

APPLICATION FOR GENEALOGICAL SEARCH

**Manitoba
Community
Services**
Vital Statistics

Please print all information clearly

B I R T H

SURNAME	GIVEN NAME(S)	SEX

SURNAME SPELLING VARIATIONS:

DATE OF BIRTH	PLACE OF BIRTH
MONTH DAY YEAR	

NAME OF FATHER (SURNAME)	GIVEN NAME(S)	MAIDEN NAME OF MOTHER (SURNAME)	GIVEN NAME(S)

D E A T H

SURNAME OF DECEASED	GIVEN NAME(S)	MARITAL STATUS

DATE OF DEATH	PLACE OF DEATH	AGE	SEX
MONTH DAY YEAR			

M A R R I A G E

NAME OF BRIDEGROOM (SURNAME)	GIVEN NAME(S)

MAIDEN SURNAME OF BRIDE	GIVEN NAME(S)

DATE OF MARRIAGE	PLACE OF MARRIAGE
MONTH DAY YEAR	

FATHER OF BRIDEGROOM	GIVEN NAME(S)	FATHER OF BRIDE	GIVEN NAME(S)

MAIDEN SURNAME OF BRIDEGROOM'S MOTHER	GIVEN NAME(S)	MAIDEN SURNAME OF BRIDE'S MOTHER	GIVEN NAME(S)

NOTES:

1. The document issued is a certified photocopy of the registration of the event on file in this office, each of which is stamped "Genealogical Purposes Only".

2. The certified photocopies contain information exactly as recorded on the original registration and, although the information may differ from your application, it cannot be amended at this time.

3. If either the party concerned or the immediate next of kin are still living, we require their permission in writing to be attached to this application.

4. The fee for search and document is   which should be paid by cheque or money order made payable to "Minister of Finance" and enclosed with this application.

I further agree that the search and information provided to me as a result of my application being approved is in fact for genealogical purposes ONLY and that the information released to me will not be or caused to be used for any unlawful or improper purposes.

Applicant's name:	My relationship to the above

Address:

City/Town:	Province:	Code:

Applicant's signature:	Telephone:

Complete this application and return to: Vital Statistics, 104 - 401 York Avenue, Winnipeg, Manitoba R3C 0P8.

MG-6874 (Rev. 85)

DEMANDE DE RECHERCHE GÉNÉALOGIQUE

Services communautaires Manitoba
État civil

Écrire clairement en lettres moulées

NAISSANCE

NOM DE FAMILLE	PRÉNOMS	SEXE

VARIATIONS ORTHOGRAPHIQUES DE NOM DE FAMILLE:

DATE DE NAISSANCE	LIEU DE NAISSANCE
JOUR MOIS ANNÉE	

NOM DE FAMILLE DU PÈRE	PRÉNOM(S)	NOM DE JEUNE FILLE DE LA MÈRE	PRÉNOM(S)

DÉCÈS

NOM DE FAMILLE DU DE LA DÉFUNT(E)	PRÉNOM(S)	ÉTAT MATRIMONIAL

DATE DU DÉCÈS	LIEU DU DÉCÈS	ÂGE	SEXE
JOUR MOIS ANNÉE			

MARIAGE

NOM DE FAMILLE DE L'ÉPOUX	PRÉNOM(S)

NOM DE JEUNE FILLE DE L'ÉPOUSE	PRÉNOM(S)

DATE DU MARIAGE	LIEU DU MARIAGE
JOUR MOIS ANNÉE	

PÈRE DE L'ÉPOUX	PRÉNOM(S)	PÈRE DE L'ÉPOUSE	PRÉNOM(S)

NOM DE JEUNE FILLE DE LA MÈRE DE L'ÉPOUX	PRÉNOM(S)	NOM DE JEUNE FILLE DE LA MÈRE DE L'ÉPOUSE	PRÉNOM(S)

REMARQUE:

1. Ce document est une photocopie authentique du document contenu dans nos dossiers, chacun d'entre eux portant la mention "Réservé à la recherche généalogique".

2. Les renseignements fournis sur les photocopies authentiques sont conformes en tous points à ceux du document original et même si certaines différences existent entre ce dernier et votre formule de demande, nous ne pouvons pas y apporter de corrections actuellement.

3. Si l'intéressé(e) ou son plus proche parent est encore vivant(e), nous leur demandons de joindre une autorisation écrite à cette demande.

4. Le coût de la recherche et du document s'élève à   . Vous pouvez payer par mandat ou chèque libellé à l'ordre du Ministre des finances et le joindre à votre demande.

Je conviens de plus que la recherche autorisée par suite de ma demande est menée strictement à des fins généalogiques et que je ne permettrai pas que les renseignements qui me seront fournis soient ou puissent être utilisés à des fins illicites ou irrégulières.

Nom de la personne qui fait la demande :	Lien de parenté avec la personne susmentionnée :
Adresse:	
Ville: Province:	Code postal:
Signature: Téléphone:	

Remplir cette demande et la renvoyer à l'adresse suivante : État civil, 401, avenue York, pièce 104, Winnipeg (Manitoba) R3C 0P8.

MG-6874 (Rév. 85)

CANADA—
Newfoundland

Send your requests to:

Vital Statistics Division
Department of Health
Confederation Building
St. John's, Newfoundland, Canada A1C 5T7

(709) 576-3308

Cost for a certified Birth Certificate	Can $10.00
Cost for a certified Marriage Certificate	Can $10.00
Cost for a certified Death Certificate	Can $10.00

The Newfoundland Department of Health has records from 1892.

Vital Statistics Division, Department of Health

APPLICATION FOR BIRTH CERTIFICATE

Last Name . . . .

. . . .

               first name   middle name

Date of birth . . . .

Place of birth . . . .

Name of Parish or Mission . . . .

Names of parents . . . .

The fee is for every certificate	Certificates required: PAPER . . . . or WALLET SIZE . . . .

Signature of Applicant . . . .

Address . . . .

Relationship to Applicant . . . .

PLEASE DO NOT WRITE BELOW THIS LINE!

This is an extract from the registration:

Name		Sex
Date	Father	
Place	Mother	
Record Number	Date of Registration	
Baptized on	By Rev.	

	Amt.	Cash Book No.
Search by Date	rec'd.	Receipt No.
Certificate No. Counter-signed by		Date

H-623
15-623-0515

APPLICATION FOR SEARCH AND CERTIFICATE—MARRIAGE

TO: Department of Health
    Vital Statistics Division
    St. John's, Newfoundland   File No. ....

I hereby apply for Search of the Records and Certificate of Marriage of...

.... and ....
                  (name of bridegroom)   (name of bride)

Month, day and year of marriage...

Place of Marriage...

Marriage was solemnized by the Rev. ....

in the .... Church.
              (denomination)

I enclose $.............................in payment of fee for .... certificates.

Signature of applicant ....

ADDRESS...

The fee is   for every certificate

REPORT ON SEARCH

PLEASE DO NOT WRITE BELOW THIS LINE!

Bridegroom		Bride	
Age	Bachelor, Widower	Age	Spinster, Widow

Date of Marriage

Place of Marriage

Marriage solemnized by

Date of Registration	Record Number

Search by	Date	Amount Received

Certificate No.	Typed by	Cash Book

H-702

APPLICATION FOR SEARCH AND CERTIFICATE—DEATH

To the Department of Health,

  Vital Statistics Division,   File No. _____

    St. John's, Newfoundland.

    I hereby apply for Search of the Records and Certificate of Death of _____

_____

                                (name of deceased)

Month, day and year of death _____

Place of Death _____

Place of burial _____

    I enclose $_____ in payment of fee for _____ certificates.

Signature of applicant _____

ADDRESS _____

The fee is   for every certificate

Report on Search

_____

_____

PLEASE DO NOT WRITE BELOW THIS LINE!

Name of deceased

Age	Sex	Date of Death
Marital Status		Place of Death
Religion		Place of Burial
Record Number		Date of Registration

Search by	Date	Amount Received
Certificate No.	Typed by	Cash Book

CANADA—
Northwest Territories

Send your requests to:

Registrar General
Vital Statistics
Government of the Northwest Territories
P.O. Box 1320
Yellowknife, Northwest Territories, Canada X1A 2L9

(403) 873-7404

Cost for a certified Birth Certificate	Can $5.00
Cost for a certified Marriage Certificate	Can $5.00
Cost for a certified Death Certificate	Can $5.00

The Northwest Territories Registrar General has records from 1925.

Northwest Territories

APPLICATION FOR CERTIFICATE
REGISTRAR GENERAL, VITAL STATISTICS
GOVERNMENT OF THE NORTHWEST TERRITORIES
YELLOWKNIFE, N.W.T. X1A 2L9

SHADED AREA FOR OFFICE USE ONLY

IF BIRTH CERTIFICATE(S) REQUIRED, COMPLETE THIS SECTION.

NAME (SURNAME, IF MARRIED WOMAN, MAIDEN SURNAME)   SEX   WALLET SIZE

DATE OF BIRTH   YR   MO   DAY   PLACE OF BIRTH (CITY, TOWN OR VILLAGE)   PAPER (21.5 cm X 28 cm)

NAME OF FATHER (SURNAME)   (GIVEN NAMES)   RESTRICTED PHOTO-COPY, SEE NOTES

MAIDEN NAME OF MOTHER (SURNAME)   (GIVEN NAMES)

REGISTRATION DATE: REGISTRATON NUMBER:

IF MARRIAGE CERTIFICATE(S) REQUIRED, COMPLETE THIS SECTION.

NAME OF BRIDEGROOM (SURNAME)   (GIVEN NAMES)   WALLET SIZE

MAIDEN NAME OF BRIDE (SURNAME)   (GIVEN NAMES)   PAPER (21.5 cm X 28 cm)

DATE OF MARRIAGE   YR   MO   DAY   PLACE OF MARRIAGE (CITY, TOWN OR VILLAGE)   RESTRICTED PHOTO-COPY, SEE NOTES

REGISTRATION DATE: REGISTRATION NUMBER:

IF DEATH CERTIFICATE(S) REQUIRED, COMPLETE THIS SECTION.

NAME OF DECEASED (SURNAME)   (GIVEN NAMES)   SEX   DEATH CERTIFICATE

DATE OF DEATH   YR   MO   DAY   PLACE OF DEATH (CITY, TOWN OR VILLAGE)

PERMANENT RESIDENCE OF DECEASED PRIOR TO DEATH

AGE   MARITAL STATUS   IF DECEASED MARRIED, GIVE NAME OF SPOUSE.

NAME OF FATHER OF DECEASED   MAIDEN NAME OF MOTHER OF DECEASED

REGISTRATION DATE: REGISTRATION NUMBER:

DO NOT DETACH. PLEASE RETURN COMPLETE SET INTACT

I REQUIRE THESE CERTIFICATE(S) FOR THE FOLLOWING REASON(S). _____

RELATIONSHIP TO PERSON NAMED _____

SIGNATURE OF APPLICANT   PHONE NUMBER BUSINESS   RESIDENCE   DATE   YR   MO   DAY   FEE ENCLOSED WITH THIS APPLICATION $

NAME

STREET ADDRESS

CITY   PROVINCE

FOR OFFICE USE ONLY.

AMOUNT RECEIVED:

REFUND/RETURN:

CANADA—
Nova Scotia

Send your requests to:

Deputy Registrar General
Nova Scotia Department of Health
P.O. Box 157
Halifax, Nova Scotia, Canada B3J 2M9

(902) 424-4380

Cost for a certified Birth Certificate	Can $10.00
Cost for a short form Birth Certificate	Can $ 5.00
Cost for a wallet size Birth Certificate	Can $ 5.00
Cost for a certified Marriage Certificate	Can $10.00
Cost for a certified Death Certificate	Can $10.00

The Nova Scotia Department of Health has birth and death records from October 1, 1908 and marriage records from 1907 to 1918 (depending on the county).

APPLICANT'S NAME:

FULL ADDRESS:

IMPORTANT:
"STATE POSTAL CODE"

PLEASE ADDRESS ALL COMMUNICATIONS TO:

Deputy Registrar General
P.O. Box 157
Halifax, Nova Scotia
B3J 2M9

NOTE: Please complete full information under appropriate section below.

I HEREBY APPLY FOR CERTIFICATE(S) AS INDICATED BELOW:

IF BIRTH CERTIFICATE(S) REQUIRED COMPLETE THIS SECTION (Please Print)	(Please ✓)
Full Name (also maiden surname)	Wallet-size
Full Date of Birth-------------	
Full Place of Birth------------	Long-form (Restricted)
Father's Full Name-------------	
Mother's Full Maiden Name------	
Specific Reason for Request----	

IF MARRIAGE CERTIFICATE(S) REQUIRED COMPLETE THIS SECTION (Please Print)	(Please ✓)
Full Name of Groom---------	Wallet-size
Full Maiden Name of Bride--	
Full Date of Marriage------	Long-form (Restricted)
Full Place of Marriage-----	
Specific Reason for Request	

IF DEATH CERTIFICATE(S) REQUIRED COMPLETE THIS SECTION (Please Print)	(Please ✓)
Full Name of Person Deceased	Short-form
Full Date of Death----------	
Full Place of Death---------	Long-form (Restricted)
Permanent Residence of Deceased Prior To Death-----	
Specific Reason for Request-	

CANADA—
Ontario

Send your requests to:

Office of the Registrar General
MacDonald Block
Parliament Buildings
Toronto, Ontario, Canada M7A 1Y5

(416) 965-1687

Cost for a certified Birth Certificate	Can $5.00
Cost for a certified Marriage Certificate	Can $5.00
Cost for a certified Death Certificate	Can $5.00

The Registrar General has records from 1869.

Office of the Registrar General
Ontario

Bureau du registraire général

Application for Certificate or Search
Demande de certificat ou de recherche

For Office Use Only
Réservé Au ministère

*Please read notes on reverse of this form

*Veuillez lire les remarques au verso

Mail Certificate to:
Poster le certificat à:

Name / Nom	
Street and No. / Rue et N°	Apt. No. / N° d'app.
City Zone Prov. / Ville Zone Prov.	Postal Code postal

Applicant - Address - If different to mailing address
Adresse du demandeur si c'est une autre personne

Name / Nom	
Street and No. / Rue et N°	Apt. No. / N° d'app.
City Zone Prov. / Ville Zone Prov.	Postal Code postal

| Today's Date / Date d'aujourd'hui | Telephone No. - Home / N° de téléphone - Domicile | Telephone No. - Business / N° de téléphone - Bureau | Fee enclosed $ / Frais inclus $ |

| State relationship to person named on certificate/solicitors see on reverse / Lien de parenté avec la personne nommée sur le certificat/avocats voir au verso | Signature of Applicant / Signature du demandeur | State reason certificate required / Motif de la demande de certificat |

*Please indicate type and number of certificates required
*Prière d'indiquer le genre et le nombre de certificats requis

BIRTH 0 NAISSANCE

Complete this part for birth certificate   0   **Remplir cette section pour un certificat de naissance**

Wallet Size / Format Poche   0
File Size / Format Dossier   1
Extended / Détaillé
Certified / Certifié   2
Genealogical (See Reverse) / Généalogique (Voir verso)   4

Last Name / Nom	First Name/Other Names / Prénoms	Sex / Sexe
Date of Birth D/J M/M Y/A / Date de naissance	Place of Birth (city, town or village) / Lieu de naissance (ville ou village)	Hospital where event ocurred - if known / Si connu, nom de l'hôpital.
Last Name of Father / Nom du père	First Name / Prénoms	Father's Birthplace / Lieu de naissance du père	Age at time of birth / Âge à la naissance
Birth Name of Mother (Last Name) / Nom de jeune fille de la mère	First Name / Prénoms	Mother's Birthplace / Lieu de naissance de la mère	Age at time of birth / Âge à la naissance

For Office Use Only
Registration Number / Numéro d'enregistrement
Registration Date / Date d'enregistrement
Réservé Au ministère

MARRIAGE 01 MARIAGE

Complete this part for marriage certificate   01   **Remplir cette section pour un certificat de mariage**

Wallet Size / Format Poche   0
File Size / Format Dossier   1
Certified / Certifié   2
Genealogical (See Reverse) / Généalogique (voir verso)   4

Last Name of Groom / Nom du marié	First Name/Other Names / Prénoms	Age at time of Marriage / Âge le jour du mariage	Groom's Father's Name / Nom du père du marié	Mother's Birth Name / Nom de jeune fille de la mère
Last Name of Bride / Nom de la mariée	First Name / Prénoms	Age at time of Marriage / Âge le jour du mariage	Bride's Father's Name / Nom du père de la mariée	Mother's Birth Name / Nom de jeune fille de la mère
Date of Marriage D/J M/M Y/A / Date du mariage	Place of marriage (City, Town or Village) / Lieu du mariage (ville ou village)			
Bridegroom's Place of Birth / Lieu de naissance du marié		Bride's Place of Birth / Lieu de naissance de la mariée		

For Office Use Only
Registration Number / Numéro d'enregistrement
Registration Date / Date d'enregistrement
Réservé Au ministère

DEATH 02 DÉCÈS

Complete this part for death certificate   02   **Remplir cette section pour un certificat de décès**

File Size / Format dossier   1
Certified / certifié   2
Genealogical (See Reverse) / Généalogique (Voir Verso)   4

Last Name of deceased / Nom du défunt	First Name/Other Names / Prénoms	Sex / Sexe
Date of Death D/J M/M Y/A / Date du décès	Place of Death (city, town or village) / Lieu de décès (ville ou village)	Hospital / Hôpital	Marital status / État matrimonial	Occupation / Profession
Permanent residence of deceased prior to death / Domicile permanent du défunt avant le décès		Age upon death / Âge au décès	Birthplace / Lieu de naissance
Father's Name / Nom du père	Father's Place of Birth / Lieu de naissance du père	Mother's Name / Nom de la mère	Mother's Place of Birth / Lieu de naissance de la mère

For Office Use Only
Registration Number / Numéro d'enregistrement
Registration Date / Date d'enregistrement
Réservé Au ministère

11076 (04/85)

I ENTITLEMENT TO CERTIFICATES/ CERTIFIED COPIES

Please note that there are restrictions as to who may obtain a certificate or certified copy of a birth or marriage registration.

The following individuals may obtain a certified copy or certificate of:

1. **BIRTH**
   a) the individual
   b) the individual's parents
   c) a solicitor representing one of the above

2. **MARRIAGE**
   a) the bride or groom
   b) parents or children of the marriage
   c) a solicitor representing one of the above

3. **GENEALOGICAL EXTRACT**

   A request for a genealogical extract by someone not entitled to a certicate will only be issued where the subjects are deceased. There are no records of events filed in the Registrar General's Office prior to 1869. Any request which does not meet the above criteria should be accompanied by written authorization from an entitled party or a written explanation as to relationship, reason for request and why authorization is not available.

II OMISSION OF INFORMATION ON REVERSE

All requests with incomplete information must be accompanied by a written explanation for the omission.

III Solicitors must clearly identify client and state specific reason for each request.

I AYANT(S) DROIT AUX CERTIFICATS/COPIES CERTIFIÉES

Veuillez noter qu'il y a des restrictions quant à savoir qui est autorisé à se procurer un certificat ou une copie certifiée d'un enregistrement de naissance ou de mariage.

Les personnes suivantes peuvent se procurer une copie certifiée ou un certificat de:

1. **NAISSANCE**
   a) la partie concernée
   b) les parents de la (des) partie(s) concernée(s)
   c) un avocat représentant l'une des personnes ci-dessus

2. **MARIAGE**
   a) le ou la marié(e)
   b) les parents ou les enfants du mariage
   c) un avocat représentant l'une des personnes ci-dessus

3. **EXTRAITS GÉNÉALOGIQUES**

   Une demande d'extrait généalogique de quelqu'un non autorisé à se procurer un certificat sera emise seulement lorsque les personnes sont décédées. Le bureau du registraire géneral ne possède pas de dossiers datant d'avant le 1er juillet 1869. Toute demande qui ne rencontre pas les critères ci-haut mentionnées devrait être accompagnée d'une autorisation écrite de la partie concernée ou d'une justification écrite du lien de parenté, la raison de la demande et pourquoi l'autorisation écrite n'est pas disponible.

II OMISSION DE RENSEIGNEMENTS AU VERSO

Toutes demandes imcomplètes de renseignements doivent être accompagnées d'une justification écrite de l'omission.

III Les avocats doivent identifier le client et déclarer la raison exacte de chaque demande.

THE FEE FOR EACH CERTIFICATE OR 5 YEAR SEARCH IS

DO NOT SEND CASH OR STAMPS AS PAYMENT BY MAIL

- The department will not be responsible for cash lost in the mail. Stamps are NOT acceptable as payment.
- For mail applications, enclose a money order or cheque made payable to:
  THE TREASURER OF ONTARIO.

- Persons living abroad should obtain an international money order in Canadian funds.

Address all applications or correspondence TO:
OFFICE OF THE REGISTRAR GENERAL,
MacDonald Block,
Parliament Buildings,
Toronto, Ontario
M7A 1Y5

LES FRAIS SONT DE   PAR CERTIFICAT OU RECHERCHE SUR 5 ANS

N'ENVOYEZ PAS D'ARGENT NI DE TIMBRES PAR LA POSTE

- *Le département n'est pas responsable de l'argent perdu dans le courrier et n'accepte pas de timbres en paiement.*
- *Pour les demandes par correspondance, joindre un chèque ou un mandat à l'ordre du:*
  TRÉSORIER DE L'ONTARIO.

- *Les personnes demeurant à l'étranger devraient acheter un mandat international en devises canadiennes.*

Adresser toutes les demandes et la correspondance AU:
BUREAU DU REGISTRAIRE GÉNÉRAL
Édifice MacDonald
Queen's Park
Toronto, (Ontario)
M7A 1Y5

CANADA—
Prince Edward Island

Send your requests to:

> Prince Edward Island
>   Department of Health & Social Services
> Division of Vital Statistics
> P.O. Box 2000
> Charlottetown, Prince Edward Island
> Canada C1A 7N8

(902) 892-1001

Cost for a certified Birth Certificate	Can $5.00
Cost for a certified Marriage Certificate	Can $5.00
Cost for a certified Death Certificate	Can $5.00

The Division of Vital Statistics has records from 1906. At this time they do not provide application forms for vital records but request that you state your request in a brief letter.

CANADA—
Quebec

Send your requests to:

Archives Nationales du Quebec
Regional Centre
1210 Ave de Seminaire
St. Foy, Quebec, Canada G1V 4N1

(418) 643-1322

Send your requests for Marriage Certificates to:

Genealogy Department
Bibliotheque de la Ville de Montreal
1210 Sherbrooke E.
Montreal, Quebec, Canada H2L 1L9

(514) 872-5923

Cost for a certified Birth Certificate	Can $5.00
Cost for a certified Marriage Certificate	Can $5.00
Cost for a certified Death Certificate	Can $5.00

Vital records are not kept in a central repository in Quebec. The Archives Nationales du Quebec and the Bibliotheque de la Ville de Montreal have extensive collections of vital records up to the 1980s. To obtain copies of vital records you should contact them or write to the parish where the event took place. There are no application forms available for this purpose.

CANADA— Saskatchewan

Send your requests to:

Province of Saskatchewan
Department of Health
Division of Vital Statistics
3475 Albert Street
Regina, Saskatchewan, Canada S4S 6X6

(306) 787-3092

Cost for a certified Birth Certificate	Can $10.00
Cost for a certified Marriage Certificate	Can $10.00
Cost for a certified Death Certificate	Can $10.00

The Saskatchewan Department of Health has records from 1878.

PROVINCE OF SASKATCHEWAN
DEPARTMENT OF HEALTH
DIVISION OF VITAL STATISTICS
3475 ALBERT ST. REGINA S4S 6X6

APPLICATION FOR CERTIFICATE

Before entering the type and number of
certificates required, please read carefully
the notes on the other side of this form.

If Birth Certificate(s) Required Complete This Section

Shaded Area For Office Use Only	Name (Surname, if married woman, maiden Surname)	(Given Names)	Sex	Wallet Size ☐ 3¾" X 2½"
	Date of Birth — Day / Month / Year	Place of Birth (City, Town or Village)		Intermediate Size ☐ 8½" X 7"
	Name of Father (Surname)	(Given Names)		Certified Photocopy ☐ 8½" X 14"
	Maiden Name of Mother (Surname)	(Given Names)		

Registration Date: Registration Number:

If Marriage Certificate(s) Required Complete This Section

Name of Bridegroom (Surname)	(Given Names)	Wallet Size ☐ 3¾" X 2½"
Maiden Name of Bride (Surname)	(Given Names)	Intermediate Size ☐ 6½" X 5½"
Date of Marriage — Day / Month / Year	Place of Marriage (City, Town or Village)	Certified Photocopy ☐ 8½" X 14"

Registration Date: Registration Number:

If Death Certificate(s) Required Complete This Section

Name of Deceased (Surname)	(Given Names)	Sex	Death Certificate ☐
Date of Death — Day / Month / Year	Place of Death (City, Town or Village)		
Permanent Residence of Deceased Prior to Death		Age	
If Deceased Married Give Name of Spouse		Marital Status	
Name of Father of Deceased	Maiden Name of Mother of Deceased		

Registration Date: Registration Number: Fee Enclosed With This Application $

Division of Vital Statistics   Saskatchewan Health

1.   My reason for requiring the certificate(s) ordered is: _____

2.   My relationship to the person named on each certificate requested is: _____

Date of Application: _____ Day / Month / Year

☐ To be mailed to:

Signature of Applicant _____

Telephone: Bus. _____ Res. _____

Name
Street
City
Pro. or Country
P. Code

Fee Received:

For Office Use Only

Amount Returned:

For Office Use Only

V.S. 17 (2-85)

CANADA—
Yukon

Send your requests to:

Deputy Registrar General of Vital Statistics
P.O. Box 2703
Whitehorse, Yukon, Canada Y1A 2C6

(403) 667-5207

Cost for a certified Birth Certificate	Can $10.00
Cost for a certified Marriage Certificate	Can $10.00
Cost for a certified Death Certificate	Can $10.00

The Registrar General has birth records from 1898 and complete records from 1925.

Yukon
Department of Health
and Human Resources

REGISTRAR GENERAL OF VITAL STATISTICS
Box 2703
Whitehorse, Yukon
Y1A 2C6

APPLICATION FOR BIRTH CERTIFICATION

I hereby apply for certification, as indicated below:

My name is: _____
(Full Name)

Please mail certification to me at:

_____
(Full Mailing Address)

1. Particulars of person whose certificate is required:

(a) NAME: _____
(Surname at BIRTH)   (Given Names)

(b) BIRTH DATE:_____ (c)PLACE OF BIRTH: _____

(d) SOCIAL INSURANCE NUMBER: _____

(e) Name of Father: _____
(Surname)   (Given Names)

(f) Mother's MAIDEN NAME: _____
(Surname)   (Given Names)

2. This certification is required for the following purposes:

_____

3. State relationship to person named in item 1: _____

4. -Wallet-sized certificates .... each
   -Certified True Copy (Court Purposes Only)..... each
   -Framed certificate (7½ x 8½)
    which includes parent(s) names and place
    of birth ....

CHEQUE OR MONEY ORDER TO BE MADE PAYABLE TO "GOVERNMENT OF YUKON"

Fee of $_____ is enclosed.

Office
Use
Only

Reg. No. _____
Reg. Date _____

_____
Written signature of Applicant

YG(1234Q)F1 Rev.01-84

Yukon
Department of Health
and Human Resources

REGISTRAR GENERAL OF VITAL STATISTICS
Box 2703
Whitehorse, Yukon
Y1A 2C6

APPLICATION FOR MARRIAGE CERTIFICATION

I hereby apply for certification, as indicated below:

My name is: _____
                                          (Full Name)

Please mail certification to me at:

_____
                    (Full Mailing Address)

---

1. Particulars:

    (a) Name of Bridegroom: _____
                              (Surname)   (Given Names)

    (b) Name of Bride: _____
                         (Surname before marriage) (Given Names)

    (c) Date of marriage: _____

    (d) Place of marriage: _____

2. This certification is required for the following purposes:

_____

3. Certificate of Marriage (Wallet-sized)........   each
    Certified True Copy of Marriage Registration..   each

CHEQUE OR MONEY ORDER MADE PAYABLE TO "GOVERNMENT OF YUKON"

Fee of $_____is enclosed.

Registration Number _____
Registration Date _____
                                  _____
                                  Written signature of Applicant

YG(851Q)Fl Rev.01/84

Yukon
Department of Health
and Human Resources

REGISTRAR GENERAL OF VITAL STATISTICS
Box 2703
Whitehorse, Yukon
Y1A 2C6

APPLICATION FOR DEATH CERTIFICATE

I hereby apply for certification, as indicated below:

My name is: _____
(Full Name)

Please mail certification to me at:

_____
(Full Mailing Address)

1. Particulars of person whose certificate is required:

   (a) NAME: _____
              (Surname)   (Given Names)

   (b) DATE OF DEATH: _____

   (c) PLACE OF DEATH: _____

2. This certification is required for the following purposes:

   _____

   _____

3. State relationship to person named in item 1: _____

4. Certificate of Death ....   each

              CHEQUE OR MONEY ORDER MADE PAYABLE TO:
              "GOVERNMENT OF THE YUKON TERRITORY"

Fee of $ _____ is enclosed.

Registration No: _____

Registration Date: _____   _____
                               Written signature of Applicant

YG(1230Q)F1 Rev.01/84

IRELAND

Send your requests to:

Registrar General
Custom House
8-11 Lombard Street East
Dublin 2, Ireland

(0001) 711000

Cost for a certified Birth Certificate	Ire £3.00
Cost for a short form Birth Certificate	Ire £1.50
Cost for a certified Marriage Certificate	Ire £3.00
Cost for a certified Death Certificate	Ire £3.00
Cost for a duplicate copy, when ordered at the same time	Ire £2.00

The Registrar General has records from 1864 and Protestant (Church of Ireland) marriages from 1845.

Seol aon fhreagra chun:—
Address any reply to:—
AN tARD CHLÁRAITHEOIR
fé'n uimhir seo:—
(quoting:—)

OIFIG AN ARD—CHLÁRAITHEORA,
8-11 SRÁID LOMBAIRD THOIR,
(8-11 Lombard Street East),
BAILE ÁTHA CLIATH, 2.
(Dublin 2).

....19....

A Chara

With reference to your application for a birth certificate the information requested below should be provided as accurately as possible and the form returned to this Office with the necessary fee. All Cheques, Postal or Money Orders should be made payable to "The Registrar General".

Mise le meas.

Ard-Chláraitheoir

_____

FEES

Full Birth Certificate (including search fee)..

Short Birth Certificate (including search fee)..

If more than one certificate relating to the birth of the same person is required an additional fee of   should be forwarded for each extra full certificate or   for each extra short certificate.

All Cheques and Postal Orders to be made payable to An tArd Chláraitheoir.

SURNAME of PERSON whose Birth Certificate is required _____

FIRST NAME(S) in full _____

Date of Birth _____

Place of Birth
(If in a town, name of street to be given) _____

Father's Name _____

Father's Occupation _____

Mother's First Name(s) and Maiden Surname _____

Has the Person whose Birth record is required been legally adopted?   Yes/No _____

Signature of Applicant..

Address...

....

Date...19.....

26B.

150242 Gr. 10.01 5m 4/85 Fodhla H338 GRO 75

Seol aon fhreagra chun:—
Address any reply to:—
AN tARD CHLÁRAITHEOIR
fé'n uimhir seo:—
(quoting:—)

OIFIG AN ARD—CHLÁRAITHEORA,
8-11 SRÁID LOMBAIRD THOIR,
(8-11 Lombard Street East),
BAILE ÁTHA CLIATH, 2.
(Dublin 2).

....19....

A Chara

With reference to your application for a marriage certificate the information requested below should be provided as accurately as possible and the form returned to this Office with the necessary fee. All Cheques, Postal or Money Orders should be made payable to "THE REGISTRAR GENERAL".

Mise le meas.

Ard-Chláraitheoir

———————————————

FEES

Marriage Certificate (including search fee)...

If more than one certificate relating to the marriage of the same person is required an additional fee of should be forwarded for each extra certificate.

NAME and ADDRESS of the Parties Married (to be written in full in each case).

(a)...

(b)...

Date of Marriage

Where Married

Signature of Applicant...

Address...

....

Date...19....

26M.

150244 Gr. 10.01 3m 4/85 Fodhla H340 GRO 75

Seol aon fhreagra chun:—
Address any reply to:—

AN tARD CHLÁRAITHEOIR

fé'n uimhir seo:—
(quoting:—)

OIFIG AN ARD—CHLÁRAITHEORA,
8-11 SRÁID LOMBAIRD THOIR,
(8-11 Lombard Street East),
BAILE ÁTHA CLIATH, 2.
(Dublin 2).

....19....

A Chara

With reference to your application for a death certificate the information requested below should be provided as accurately as possible and the form returned to this Office with the necessary fee. All Cheques, Postal or Money Orders should be made payable to "THE REGISTRAR GENERAL".

Mise le meas.

Ard-Chláraitheoir

FEES

Death Certificate (including search fee)...

If more than one certificate relating to the death of the same person is required an additional fee of should be forwarded for each extra certificate.

SURNAME of DECEASED

FIRST NAME(S) in full

Date of Death

Place of Death
(If in a town, name of street to be given)

Age of Deceased

Occupation of Deceased

State whether Single, Married, Widow, Widower

Signature of Applicant...

Address...

....

Date...19.....

26D.

150243 Cr. 10.01 3m 4/85 Fodhla H339 GRO 75

UNITED KINGDOM—
England and Wales

Send your requests to:

General Register Office
St. Catherine's House
10 Kingsway
London WC2B 6JP, England

01-242-0262

Cost for a certified Birth Certificate	£10.00
Cost for a short form Birth Certificate	£ 7.50
Cost for a certified Marriage Certificate	£10.00
Cost for a certified Death Certificate	£10.00

The General Register Office has records from July 1, 1837.

APPLICATION FOR BIRTH CERTIFICATE

General Register Office, St. Catherines House, 10 Kingsway, London WC2B 6JP

Please allow   days for despatch of certificates

Requirements

.... Full certificate(s) at   each

.... Short certificate(s) at   each   £_____

amount received

Please tick appropriate box:

☐ Birth Register

☐ Adoption Register

Particulars of the person whose certificate is required. Remember, we need full details to ensure a positive search.

Surname
Forenames
Date of birth
Place of birth
Fathers surname
Fathers forenames
Mothers maiden surname
Mothers forenames

Applicant

Mr/Mrs/Miss	
Full postal address	

Notes

This Office holds records of births registered in England and Wales since 1st July 1837.

If you attend St Catherines House, and make the search personally the certificate is then usually ready after 48 hours. The fees are   for a full certificate or   for a short certificate.

You can also obtain certificates at the same fee on application in person or by post to the Superintendent Registrar for the district where the birth occurred.

Short Certificate – shows only the name, sex, date of birth and place of birth.

Full Certificate – This is a full copy of the birth entry, and includes particulars of parentage and registration.

Adoption Certificate – the full certificate is a copy of the entry with the date of birth, particulars of the adoption and the adoptive parent or parents; a short certificate bears no reference to adoption.

Cheques, postal orders, etc should be made payable to **"The Registrar General"**. Payment from abroad may be made by cheque, international money order, or draft, in favour of the Registrar General. Orders, cheques and drafts should always be expressed in Sterling.

If we cannot find the entry, after a two year search either side of the date given, a fee of £6.00 will be retained, whether the application is for a full or short certificate, and the balance returned.

FOR OFFICE USE ONLY

CAS	
Amount received	
Fees Certificates	
Full	
Total charge	
Refund	
Desp'd	

Qtr/Year	Vol	Restricted to				
		D/S				
Page	Entry	Year	M	J	S	D
		Year	M	J	S	D
District		Year	M	J	S	D
Sub-District		Year	M	J	S	D
LB MB CB MD City of County of		Year	M	J	S	D

Address label (please use BLOCK LETTERS)
Enter in this space the name and full postal address to which the certificate should be sent

APPLICATION FOR MARRIAGE CERTIFICATE

General Register Office, St. Catherines House, 10 Kingsway, London WC2B 6JP

Please allow   days for despatch of certificates

Requirements

.... certificate(s) at   each

amount received

£_____

Particulars of the person(s) whose certificate is required. Remember, we need full details to ensure a positive search.

Man's Surname	
Forenames	
Woman's Surname	
Forenames	
Date of marriage	
Place of marriage	
Name of man's father	
Name of woman's father	

Applicant

Mr/Mrs/Miss	
Full	
postal	
address	

Notes

This Office holds records of marriages registered in England and Wales since 1st July 1837.

If you attend St Catherines House, and make the search personally the certificate is then usually ready after 48 hours. The fee is

You can also obtain certificates at the same fee on application in person or by post to the Officiating minister of the church where the marriage took place or to the Superintendent Registrar of the same district.

Cheques, postal orders, etc should be made payable to **"The Registrar General"**. Payment from abroad may be made by cheque, international money order, or draft, in favour of the Registrar General. Orders, cheques and drafts should always be expressed in Sterling.

If we cannot find the entry, after a two year search either side of the date given, a fee of £6.00 will be retained.

FOR OFFICE USE ONLY

CAS	
Amount received	
Fees Certificates	
Full	
Total charge	
Refund	
Desp'd	

Qtr/Year	Vol	Restricted to				
		D/S				
Page	Entry	Year	M	J	S	D
		Year	M	J	S	D
District		Year	M	J	S	D
		Year	M	J	S	D
LB MB CB MD City of County of		Year	M	J	S	D

Address label (please use BLOCK LETTERS)
Enter in this space the name and full postal address to which the certificate should be sent

APPLICATION FOR DEATH CERTIFICATE

General Register Office, St. Catherines House, 10 Kingsway, London WC2B 6JP

Please allow   **days for despatch of certificates**

Requirements

.... certificate(s) at   each

amount
received

£_____

Particulars of the person whose certificate is required. Remember, we need full details to ensure a positive search.

Surname	
Forename(s)	
Date of death	
Place of death	
Age at death	
Occupation of Deceased	
Marital status of Deceased (if female)	

Applicant

Mr/Mrs/Miss	
Full	
postal	
address	

Notes

This Office holds records of deaths registered in England and Wales since 1st July 1837.

If you attend St Catherines House, and make the search personally the certificate is then usually ready after 48 hours. The fee is

You can also obtain certificates at the same fee on application in person or by post to the Superintendent Registrar of the district where the death occurred.

Cheques, postal orders, etc should be made payable to **"The Registrar General"**. Payment from abroad may be made by cheque, international money order, or draft, in favour of the Registrar General. Orders, cheques and drafts should always be expressed in Sterling.

If we cannot find the entry, after a two year search either side of the date given, a fee of £6.00 will be retained.

FOR OFFICE USE ONLY

CAS	
Amount received	
Fees Certificates	
Full	
Total charge	
Refund	
Desp'd	

Qtr/Year	Vol	Restricted to				
		D/S				
Page	Entry	Year	M	J	S	D
		Year	M	J	S	D
District		Year	M	J	S	D
Sub-District		Year	M	J	S	D
		Year	M	J	S	D
LB MB CB MD City of County of						

Address label (please use BLOCK LETTERS)
Enter in this space the name and full postal address to which the certificate should be sent

UNITED KINGDOM—
Northern Ireland

Send your requests to:

General Register Office
Department of Health and Social Services
Oxford House
49-55 Chichester Street
Belfast BT1 4HL, Northern Ireland

(0232) 235211

Cost for a certified Birth Certificate	£3.75
Cost for a short form Birth Certificate	£2.25
Cost for a certified Marriage Certificate	£3.75
Cost for a certified Death Certificate	£3.75
Cost for a duplicate copy, when ordered at the same time	£2.50

The General Register Office has birth and death records from January 1, 1864. Marriage records are on file from April 1, 1845 with Roman Catholic marriage records beginning on January 1, 1864.

APPLICATION FOR A
SEARCH/BIRTH CERTIFICATE

To: The Registrar General,
Oxford House, 49 - 55 Chichester Street,
Belfast BT1 4HL. (Tel. No. 235211)

FOR OFFICIAL USE

Serial No. .... Date ....

Related Nos.

Entry Ref. ....

FIRST COMPLETE PART A THEN FILL IN WHICHEVER OTHER PART REFERS TO THE TYPE OF CERTIFICATE YOU REQUIRE

A

PLEASE USE BLOCK CAPITALS

Name of Applicant
Mr.
Mrs. ....
Miss.
(STATE NAME IN FULL)

Full postal address ....

.... Tele. No ....

I enclose cheque/postal order for £ ....

Date .... Signature ....

PARTICULARS OF THE PERSON WHOSE CERTIFICATE IS REQUIRED

1. BIRTH REGISTER

USE PART 2 INSTEAD IF A CERTIFICATE FROM THE ADOPTED CHILD-REN REGISTER IS REQUIRED

Full Name at Birth	Father's Full Name	Mother's Full Name
Christian or Forenames	Christian or Forenames	Christian or Forenames
Surname	Surname	Surname
Date of Birth		Maiden Surname
Place of Birth		Mother's Residence at time of Birth

2. ADOPTED CHILD-REN REGISTER

THIS DATES FROM 1 JULY 1930 ONLY

Particulars of Adopted Person	Name(s) of Adopter(s)	Particulars of Adoption Order
Christian or Forenames	Christian or Forenames	Name of Court which made the Adoption Order
Surname	Surname	
Date of Birth		Date of the Order

B

Full Certificate

I require .... full certificate(s).
(Number)

C

Short Certificate

I require .... short certificate(s).
(Number)

D

Certificate for the Purposes of the Friendly Societies Acts

I require .... certificate(s) for the following Registered Friendly Society:

....

E

Certificate for certain other statutory purposes

I require a certificate for each undermentioned purpose against which I have placed a cross.

STATUTORY PURPOSE OF CERTIFICATE	INSERT X IF REQD	STATUTORY PURPOSE OF CERTIFICATE	INSERT X IF REQD
Child Benefit Order		Government Annuities	
Education & Libraries Order		National Savings Bank	
Electoral Law Act		Premium Savings Bonds	
Factories Act		Savings Contract	
Shops Act		Trustee Savings Bank	
Social Security Act		Ulster Savings Certificates	
		War & National Savings Certificates	

G.R.O. 40

FIRST SEARCH

Result ....

....

Date .... Searched by ....

CHECK SEARCH

Result ....

....

Date .... Searched by ....

Notes

....

....

....

....

....

Entry to be Offered	Action Taken
....	....
....	....
....	....
....	....
....	....
....	....

Fees Payable

Number	£	p	
..........Full @	....		Checked by ....
..........Short @................................	....		Date ....
..........Stat Purposes @........................	....		Stamped by ....
Total	_____		Date ....

	£	p.
In	:	
	:	

	£	p.
Out	:	
	:	
	:	

By ....

Recd. ....

Cashier ....

Date ....

By ....

Receipt

Dmd. 8873099 10/85 80M TPC 7336 Gp. 173

APPLICATION FOR A
SEARCH/MARRIAGE CERTIFICATE

To: The Registrar General,
Oxford House, 49 - 55 Chichester Street,
Belfast BT1 4HL. (Tel. No. 235211)

FOR OFFICIAL USE

Serial No. .... Date ....

Related Nos. ....

Entry Ref. ....

PLEASE COMPLETE PARTS A & B

A

PLEASE USE BLOCK CAPITALS

Name of Applicant
Mr.
Mrs. ....
Miss.   (STATE NAME IN FULL)

Full postal address ....

.... Tele. No ....

I enclose cheque/postal order for ....

Date .... Signature ....

MAN	WOMAN	Any other surname before this marriage
Surname	Maiden Surname	
Christian or Forenames	Christian or Forenames	

PLACE OF MARRIAGE	DATE OF MARRIAGE		
Full Address	Day	Month	Year

B

I require .... certificate(s).
(Number)

GRO 42

FOR OFFICIAL USE   MARRIAGE

FIRST SEARCH

Result ....
....

Date ....Searched by...............................

CHECK SEARCH

Result ....
....

Date ....Searched by...............................

Notes

....
....
....
....
....

Entry to be Offered	Action Taken
....	....
....	....
....	....
....	....
....	....
....	....

Fees Payable

Number   £   p

................Full @..

Checked by ....

Date ....

Stamped by ....

Date ....

Total _____

	£	p.
In	:	
	:	

By ....

Recd. ....

Cashier ....

Date ....

By ....

	£	p.
Out	:	
	:	
	:	

Receipt

Dmd.8372440 12/82 20M TPC 5883 Gp.173

APPLICATION FOR A
SEARCH/DEATH CERTIFICATE

To: The Registrar General,
Oxford House, 49 - 55 Chichester Street,
Belfast BT1 4HL. (Tel. No. 235211)

FOR OFFICIAL USE

Serial No. .... Date ....

Related Nos. ....

Entry Ref. ....

FIRST COMPLETE PART A THEN FILL IN WHICHEVER OTHER PART REFERS TO THE TYPE OF CERTIFICATE YOU REQUIRE

A

PLEASE USE BLOCK CAPITALS

Name of Applicant
Mr.
Mrs. ....
Miss.   (STATE NAME IN FULL)

Full postal address .... Tele. No. ....

I enclose cheque/postal order for ....

Date .... Signature ....

PARTICULARS OF THE PERSON WHOSE CERTIFICATE IS REQUIRED

Christian or Forenames

Surname

Date of Death

Place of Death	Usual Residence

Date of Birth, or age at Death

If person was married or widowed at time of death - Name of Spouse

If Death occured in last three years,
was Death reported to Coroner?

B

Full Certificate

I require .... full cerificate(s).
    (Number)

C

Certificate for purposes of Friendly Societies Acts

I require .... certificate(s) for the following Registered Friendly Society:
    (Number)

....

D

CERTIFICATE FOR CERTAIN OTHER STATUTORY PURPOSES

I require a certificate for each undermentioned purpose against which I have placed a cross.

STATUTORY PURPOSE OF CERTIFICATE	INSERT X IF REQD.	STATUTORY PURPOSE OF CERTIFICATE	INSERT X IF REQD.
Child Benefit Order		National Savings Bank	
Social Security Act		Premuim Savings Bonds	
Government Annuities		Trustee Savings Bank	
Saving Contracts		Ulster Savings Certificates	
		War & National Savings Certificates	

G.R.O. 41

FOR OFFICIAL USE   DEATH

FIRST SEARCH   Result ....

....

Date ....Searched by...

CHECK SEARCH

Result ....

....

Date ....Searched by...

Notes

....

....

....

....

....

Entry to be Offered	Action Taken
....	....
....	....
....	....
....	....
....	....
....	....

Fees Payable

Number	£	p		Checked by ....
................Full @..........................	....			Date ....
	....			Stamped by ....
................Stat Purposes @	....			Date ....
Total				

	£	p.
In	:	
	:	

Out	:
	:
	:

By ....

Recd. ....

Cashier ....

Date ....

By ....

Receipt

Dmd. 8372439 1182 20M TPC 5880 Gp.173

UNITED KINGDOM—
Scotland

Send your requests to:

General Register Office for Scotland
New Register House
Edinburgh EH1 3YT, Scotland

(031) 556-3952

Cost for a certified Birth Certificate	£5.00
Cost for a short form Birth Certificate	£2.50
Cost for a certified Marriage Certificate	£5.00
Cost for a certified Death Certificate	£5.00
Cost for a duplicate copy, when ordered at the same time	£2.50

The Registrar General has records from 1855.

GENERAL REGISTER OFFICE FOR SCOTLAND

Records Section
New Register House Edinburgh EH1 3YT
Telephone 031-556 3952 ext

To:

Date

Dear

Your letter has been returned to you for the following reason(s):-

There was not enough information to trace the entry. Please complete the application overleaf and return it to this office; and/or

No/insufficient money was enclosed to cover the cost.

Please indicate in the appropriate box(es) below the number of extracts or certificates required.

1. ☐ Abbreviated certificate of birth. This shows the person's name, surname, sex, date and place of birth. Not applicable to records before 1855.　　　Cost £

2. ☐ Extract of Birth. This is a full copy of the entry in the birth register and is used for all purposes.　　　Cost £

3. ☐ Extract of Death　　　Cost £

4. ☐ Extract of Marriage　　　Cost £

5. ☐ Extract of Divorce　　　Cost £

If more than one copy of the same entry is ordered at the same time, the fee for the second and subsequent extract is £

Cheques and postal orders should be crossed and made payable to "The Registrar General". Overseas applicants should include airmail postage. International Reply Coupons are not acceptable as payment.

All refunds will be made by sterling cheque. It is uneconomic to refund small amounts, and amounts under　　will not therefore be refunded.

Yours sincerely

Note:
When a decree of divorce was granted by the Court of Session, it was formerly the practice to enter a note on the marriage entry to show that the marriage had ended in divorce. This practice was discontinued on 1 May 1984. Where a divorce was notified to the Registrar General on or after that date, there will be no note regarding divorce on the corresponding marriage entry or on any extract of the entry.

Evidence of divorce is obtainable either from the Court where the decree was granted or from the General Register Office, New Register House, Edinburgh EH1 3YT.

*Delete as appropriate

*BIRTH

*Surname at Birth/Adoption

Forenames

*MALE/FEMALE

Place (town or parish) in which Birth occurred (adopted persons please state date of adoption, if known)

*PARENTS/ADOPTIVE PARENTS

Father's surname

Father's forenames

Mother's maiden surname

Mother's forenames

Date of Birth		
DAY	MONTH	YEAR

Date of application ....

Signature ....

*MARRIAGE/DIVORCE

Groom's surname

Forenames

Bride's surname

Forenames

Place (town or parish) in which Marriage occurred

Widow or Divorcee please state former married name

Date of Marriage		
DAY	MONTH	YEAR

Date of Divorce (if applicable)		
DAY	MONTH	YEAR

Date of application ....

Signature ....

*DEATH

Surname

Forenames

Age at Death

Place (town or parish) in which Death occurred

*PARENTS/ADOPTIVE PARENTS

Father's surname

Father's forenames

Mother's maiden surname

Mother's forenames

Date of Death		
DAY	MONTH	YEAR

Date of application ....

Signature ....

FOR OFFICE USE

R.D. No.	Year	Entry No.
RCE		

R.D. No.	Year	Entry No.
RCE		

R.D. No.	Year	Entry No.
RCE		

Notes

Notes

Notes

2572

Notes

Notes

Notes

DISCARDED

Brooks - Cork Library

Midwest
PO 71473
829.76
5/4/10

P9-AOT-748

Giants of Japan

Brooks - Cork Library
Shelton State
Community College

DISCARDED

GIANTS
of JAPAN

*The Lives of Japan's
Greatest Men and Women*

Mark Weston

KODANSHA INTERNATIONAL
New York Tokyo London

Permissions and credits appear on page 361.

On the front cover (top row): Fukuzawa Yukichi, Ariyoshi Sawako, Ibuse Masuji, Minamoto no Yoritomo, Kawabata Yasunari, Kato Shidzue. (bottom): Matsushita Konosuke, Sen no Rikyu, Ozu Yasujiro, Ueshiba Morihei, Hayashi Fumiko, Mishima Yukio.

On the back cover (top): Iwasaki Yataro, Lady Murasaki, Katsushika Hokusai, Toyotomi Hideyoshi, Tojo Hideki, Oe Kenzaburo. (bottom): Morita Akio, Matsuo Basho, Prince Shotoku, Oda Nobunaga, Emperor Hirohito, Kurosawa Akira.

Kodansha America, Inc.
575 Lexington Avenue, New York, New York 10022, U.S.A.

Kodansha International Ltd.
17-14 Otowa 1-chome, Bunkyo-ku, Tokyo 112-8652, Japan

Published in 1999 by Kodansha America, Inc.

Copyright © 1999 by Mark Weston. All rights reserved.

LIBRARY OF CONGRESS CATALOGING-IN-PUBLICATION DATA
Weston, Mark.
Giants of Japan : the lives of Japan's greatest men and women / Mark Weston.
p.   cm.
Includes index.
ISBN 1-56836-286-2 (hc)
1. Japan—Biography.   I. Title.
CD1833.W47   1999
920.052—dc21
[b]   99-11835

TEXT DESIGN BY JENNY DOSSIN